when your
baby cries

To my mother Jocelyn and my sister Elizabeth.
With love.

when your baby cries

10 rules for soothing fretful babies*
*(and their parents!)

Deborah Jackson

pinter & martin

PINTER & MARTIN

When your baby cries
10 rules for soothing fretful babies (and their parents!)

Copyright © 2004/2009 by Deborah Jackson

First published in Great Britain in 2004 by Hodder and Stoughton.
This edition first published by Pinter & Martin Ltd 2009

The right of Deborah Jackson to be identified as the Author
of the Work has been asserted by her in accordance with the
Copyright, Designs and Patents Act 1988

ISBN 978-1-905177-25-7

A CIP catalogue record for this title is
available from the British Library

Typeset in Sabon

Printed and bound in Great Britain by
Athenaeum Press Ltd, Gateshead, Tyne & Wear

This book has been printed on paper that is sourced and
harvested from sustainable forests and is FSC accredited

Pinter & Martin Ltd
6 Effra Parade
London SW2 1PS

www.pinterandmartin.com

Contents

Foreword

One Saturday early in the new millennium, sometime before I was commissioned to write this book, I was giving a parenting workshop in a trendy part of London. I'd worked at the venue before and always enjoyed the relaxed, bean-bag atmosphere and open-heartedness of the parents who took part.

So I hadn't expected the first question of the morning. It came from a father who was sitting on the carpet cradling his newborn baby.

'Why,' he said with a twinkle in his eye, 'does Gina Ford sell more books than you?'

It was a bold opener which gave an unexpected energy to our first discussion. I knew that, though the question was deliberately provocative, it would plunge us into a relevant debate. Here we were, a set of intelligent, independent-minded people, keen to enjoy the challenging process of becoming parents and ready to learn from our own experiences and mistakes. Yet many of our equally intelligent friends were in the thrall of a detailed infant timetable.* What's more it was a bestseller.

It's all too easy as a parent to be judgemental about other

---

* Gina Ford 'The Contented Little Baby: The simple secrets of calm, confident parenting', Vermilion 2001 methods of childrearing – and even easier for one childcare author to take a pot shot at an apparent rival. I never wanted to start the battle of the babycare gurus. But as a non-prescriptive writer myself, I can't ignore the recent success of highly-prescriptive advice books.

In most aspects of modern life, we prefer to be left to our own devices. Yet here was evidence that detailed directives were helpful for many new parents. Parenting by numbers (eg 8am, 10.30am, 12 noon...) was obviously a formula that sold well and – love it or hate it – I needed to understand why.

My own approach has always been to offer research rather than rules. Years of studying families from other cultures and from our own human history taught me that there's no single way to raise a baby. As many years spent bringing up my own three, delightful but very different, children reinforced the message that one size, however 'simple', simply cannot fit all. My aim as a writer was to inform and to reassure – and to promote people's individual parenting styles within a broad framework of loving care.

After the workshop, I came away with a list of supplementary questions for myself... Why have the keywords of modern childcare become DO and DON'T? Have we become so inexperienced as baby-handlers that we need nannying ourselves? Might there even be a causal relationship between the amount of advice we get from newspapers, books and interfering relatives – and the amount of guilt we wallow in every day? *Why are we prepared to succeed or fail by a stranger's set of rules?*

I decided to slip under the radar and find out. I would write a childcare manual which had all the hallmarks of a modern rulebook, but none of the dogma. My previous book – Baby Wisdom, a survey of parenting practices through time and around the world – was, admittedly, as big as a butcher's doorstop. When Your Baby Cries would be easier for new parents to pick up, put down and throw out of the window in moments of stress. I would distil the long evolution of human baby rearing into a format that busy parents would have time to digest.

And here it is, the handbook made to soothe parents as much as their offspring. Its collected wisdoms are served in 10 short chapters: rules if you prefer. These rules may not tell you what to do every minute of the day, but they do legitimately cover the important facts about infant crying. They also include a few dos and don'ts for those who like a proper set of instructions with their human delivery.

You won't be told when to draw back the curtains or put your baby down to nap, but you will be urged to relax, try out new ideas, have fun, give generously and give in. You'll get ideas for reducing your baby's crying and methods of coping, but very little to make you feel guilty or inadequate. And I defy you to find any advice that could come between you and your own, unique child.

Because in *my* book, early parenting doesn't work like that. Caring for a baby is an ancient, tactile, human activity which should be more about families getting to know each other than obeying the invisible childcare guru. I can't be there when your baby cries, but luckily your baby's not remotely interested in me. You are the only rule that matters.

Deborah Jackson, May 2009

rule one

Relax

Welcome to the baby club

You are bewildered and exhausted. Your body clock is out
of synch with your brain and you can't remember the last
time you had a decent night's sleep. Everyone tells you how
lucky you are and you know you should be celebrating, but
sometimes you feel like screaming instead. Welcome to the
baby club.

Babies are wonderful creatures, designed to give and
receive an enormous amount of pleasure. They are programmed to feed and sleep, rest and play whenever they feel
like it. They seek satisfaction through human contact and
would very much like to be carried, stroked and generally
jogged around all day. Their demands are few, but they are
constant. 'Please,' they seem to say, 'take me with you.
Never let me go.'

Fearful that babies will take over their lives, some
parents try to train them into early obedience. Popular
childcare manuals describe the drill: even the youngest
baby is expected to sleep alone; to wait for feeds; to cry
without receiving comfort. Babies (we are told) need to
learn to separate, to be patient, to postpone their desires.
Many experts insist that if you don't curb your baby's
demands today, you can expect stormy weather tomorrow.

7

And, as everyone knows, baby training means more crying.

But however keen on his or her own method, no expert is going to come and live in your house and do the training for you. The trials of baby-coaching are left to you. You are expected to cope by yourself, without practical or emotional assistance. Just to make things really difficult, we post-industrialized parents do not live in supportive communities, but isolated in flats and houses. We may not bring our babies into work, or into any place where they might make a noise. Even shops and public transport seem to be designed to keep children at bay.

If you are a first-time parent, you may (like me when I started out) have very little experience of handling babies. What you really crave is encouragement and tolerance. What you often get, unfortunately, is a queue of friends and strangers who think it's their duty to tell you you're doing it all wrong.

And you wonder why your baby cries . . .

Did you know?

Babies are born with a crying reflex, but not a laughing reflex. While giggling and laughing are useful for social interplay and attracting attention, crying is essential for survival. The aim is to bring someone running in an emergency.

What does it all mean?

As soon as the crying starts, adults typically react like a team of interpreters at the United Nations. Most of us like to have a guess at what a crying baby is 'trying to say'. We may think we are being helpful, but ordinary sentences will never be enough to sum up the sensations of a new baby. He is operating at a pre-verbal level, a stage at which he smiles with his whole face and cries from the top of his head right down to his scrunched-up toes.

Do you know what a baby's crying really means? It's a pre-verbal stab at something as unfinished and simple as:

'I feel like a . . .'

That's all. This may not sound like a proper sentence, but how could it be? Human brains are not born ready to formulate paragraphs, dish out blame or demand buttered toast and clean sheets. The only thing they can do is initiate a body-level conversation with those around them – and seek a body-level response. Our physical answers to the baby's unfinished questions teach him about the ways of the world; about what it is to be loved. As soon as he finds physical comfort or relief, his crying will stop.

It's easy to be thrown by the interpretations and interference of well-meaning friends and relations. Many people believe they are being helpful when they intrude with their personal opinions, often without any prompting. New parents simply have to realize that, although others may seem confident of their facts and certain that they have the answers, a strongly held opinion may be little more than strongly held prejudice.

And hard on the heels of diagnosis comes the cure: 'What that baby needs is . . . !' Unless you have actually asked for advice, such intrusions can be unsettling. It's particularly tough when the advice comes as criticism, or happens to undermine your own beliefs and methods.

Luckily, there is no rule saying you must always make sense or justify your actions to every would-be baby whisperer. Often the best response is to show genuine interest in your critics' concerns – why are they bothered by your choices? What is making them feel so uncomfortable or insecure?

And while you are at it, remember that all standard babycare guidance (including mine) must be reshaped to make it work for you. Attempting to parent by a set of rigid laws is like trying to carry custard in a colander – it creates an awful mess and you're left to clear it up. The current frenzy for rulebooks is just a smokescreen for our general nervousness around babies. Even the best ideas need to be pummelled into shape.

Did you know?

Many cultural groups consider it impolite to bombard new parents with babycare advice. In rural Malaysia, for instance, traditional midwives will not offer an opinion unless it is specifically requested.

Guilt-edged Emotions

There are thousands of excuses for wallowing in parental guilt: mothers feel bad about a difficult birth or breastfeeding experience; fathers feel guilty that they are often absent or not as involved as they would like. Some wish they weren't a single parent – others wish they were. Parents waste time worrying that they are too old, too young, inexperienced or past it. We become preoccupied about the past and traumatized about the future . . . tickets for the guilt trip are on sale in every home.

You may be anxious that you're all your baby's got, but believe it, *you are all your baby needs.* Your arms are better for sleeping in than any safety-checked cot; the feel of your skin is more precious than the finest silk; your voice is the first music your newborn baby wants to hear.

Some childcare experts call this the quality of being 'good

enough'. I would go further and say that – given the right support – you have all the qualities to become the practically perfect parent.

Give yourself time. Sometimes feelings of guilt can be a useful prompt that you are unhappy with aspects of your own babycare style. If this really is the case, consider whether you might like to make some changes. But all too often, guilt is that vague left-over feeling that we could have done better in the past – and this sensation can easily hamper your power to parent in the present.

Try to let past problems go and begin again with every new day. This, after all, is exactly how babies and small children approach life's hurdles and milestones. If you could only see yourself from the outside. You'd know you are doing fine.

Did you know?

An American study found that the average person spends up to two hours a day feeling guilty. Researchers say many people typically feel so guilty that for half an hour or more they are unable to function properly.

It isn't personal

Why does a crying baby make us feel so bad? For many parents, the emotions aroused by their baby's tears send them into a downward spiral of misery. If we could wade through the murky waters of a parent's mind over the course of a difficult day, we might find something like this:

He needs his nappy changing; He must be thirsty; He's ill; There's nothing wrong with him; There's something wrong with me; He's doing it deliberately; He's got me round his little finger; I can't cope; I'll never be able to cope . . .

It is so easy for the isolated parent to over-identify with the pain and frustration of the crying baby. See how the chain reaction leaves her feeling inadequate and convinced that she is unequal to the task of caring. Crying throws up confused messages that may start to scratch away at our self-esteem. And when crying persists, parents start to interpret deeper meanings than the baby ever intended:

She's too hot; She's tired; She wants me all the time; She's hungry again; She wants to be left alone; No she doesn't; I need a break; She's so naughty; There's something wrong with her; My milk isn't good enough; I'm not good enough; I'll never be good enough . . .

Babies have no idea that their primitive cries persecute their parents in this way. They don't realize that constant wailing and screaming might be counter-productive. A newborn baby is simply reacting with one of the strongest reflexes he has been given. Even older babies who have practised and so 'learnt' to cry may still not know why they do.

Your baby's crying is not personal. Don't let anyone try to suggest otherwise. It's not a reflection of the dire state of your parenting skills, a condemnation of your ability to nurture, or confirmation of your own worst fears. It's just the beginning of a sentence which will take you both a lifetime to complete.

Did you know?

Researchers have identified a number of family factors
that contribute to persistent crying in babies. These
include strains in the parents' relationship; mothers'
low self-esteem and post-natal depression. It works
both ways, of course – if your baby is persistently
crying, then you are more likely to suffer from all of
the above . . .

Your baby is unique

Your baby is a one-off. He may be governed by a bundle of
reflexes, but from birth, he also has a budding personality.
In scientific terms, we know that the human brain fires on
150 chemicals, each one in a slightly different concentration
from the next. Your baby's personal chemical levels help to
determine whether he is more or less active, more or less
anxious, more or less at ease with himself and his strange
new world. And – more or less – whether he is prone to
tears.

But genes are not and never will be the whole of the
human story. Almost all personal characteristics – even
obviously hereditary traits – are affected by the environment. For example, your child's height is hardwired into his
system, but only within a range of several inches. His final
stature will vary according to his diet, his health, the
traumas he experiences, his activity levels and, amazingly,
the climate around him.

Even a newborn baby is shaped by the environment.
(And environment doesn't mean the colour of the nursery!)
He already has a full nine months or more of gathered

experiences, from the surroundings of the womb, through the incredible shift of birth, to the day-to-day care he has received since he was born.

When we consider that personality and brain patterns are still very fluid in the first few months and years of life, we can say that these pre- and post-natal experiences are helping to turn your baby into the child and adult he will one day become. Some researchers call this the period of 'primal health'. Everything you do with your baby in the early months is helping to set his levels of well-being and shape his reactions to the world.

How does this relate to crying? Well, it's important to keep a balanced view before making any judgments on your baby's personality. It's tempting to imagine that a crotchety baby is the result of some 'crotchety' gene and that little Barney's ability to scream is related to his Great-uncle Barnaby's legendary temper (even though Great-uncle Barnaby is long dead). In reality, little Barney is still learning how to be himself – his temper will only be set in concrete if you convince yourself and others that it is so. There really are things you can do to help minimize his distress and teach him to cry less.

Never lose sight of the fact that your very original baby is open to change and that – through his relationship with you – he will be able to develop healthy patterns and fulfil his every potential.

Did you know?

Long before they are able to crawl, babies can tell the difference between a happy face and a sad one – they can even imitate facial expressions. Babies are highly receptive to our expectations

---

Get in touch

So how should you get to know your own, highly individual baby? When adults meet for the first time, they engage in 'small talk'. With a baby, the simplest, fastest and easiest way to communicate is through 'small touch', the gentle caresses and minute interactions which help you and your baby to connect.

You may be amazed to learn that mothers and fathers unconsciously touch a new baby in the same way on first meeting. This involves exploring the tiny fingers before moving across to the palms of the baby's hands, down the arms, along the legs and finally around the baby's trunk. It is one of the untaught processes which have convinced scientists of the existence of maternal and paternal instincts.

Given her newborn baby to hold, a mother tends to cradle him to the left-hand side (see Rule Nine: *Heart to heart*) and offer the breast, stroking him all the while and gazing into his eyes. The intense attraction of mother and newborn is mutual. They are both high on hormones after the birth. If left to lie on his mother's stomach, a newborn will actually initiate his first feed, crawling slowly to the nipple all by himself. The drive to connect is mysterious and powerful – and it is the impulse behind much of the crying that is to come. It is through touch that your baby wants to communicate. He craves skin-to-skin contact as much as he craves his mother's milk and he'll do anything to get it.

Skin-to-skin contact not only helps to pacify babies, it also helps to create stronger, more confident and satisfied parents. Experiments with premature babies in Colombia, South America, showed remarkable results when the infants were held skin-to-skin on their parents' chests instead of being placed in an incubator. This so-called 'Kangaroo Care' method became famous for the number of infant lives that were saved. But less well documented was the benefit it brought to anxious parents.

Nursing staff reported that mothers cried with joy as they cuddled their micro-premature newborns, declaring that it felt as though their babies had been born again. Fathers, too, were affected. After holding his baby closely for the first time, one delighted dad said, 'I feel pregnant now.'

This connection, this uninhibited delight, is precisely the kind of boost that every nervous new parent needs. I wish someone had told me how incredibly calming and confidence-building it would be to hold my first newborn next to me in this way. 'Small touch' is the beginning of intimacy. And the subtle conversation of skin-touching, practised from the start, will eventually reduce the need for crying.

Did you know?

Skin-to-skin contact helps a baby maintain his ideal body temperature, which is more than an electronic incubator could ever do. Holding a baby upright also clears his passageways for breathing – he is very comfortable in this position. Daily holding is a great idea for helping new fathers to bond.

Rule One in a nutshell

- Relax. Don't set standards so high that you will never meet them: ordinary people make practically perfect parents.
- Crying is not a personal rebuke – it is just the baby's attempt at communicating with a perplexing new world.
- Listen to advice if it pleases you, but take unwanted criticism lightly.
- Do not allow nagging guilt, ridiculous rules or feelings of failure to come between you and your baby.
- One simple way to encourage positive feelings is to hold your baby next to your skin.
- Don't assume that your crying baby is programmed to be trouble: for the first year of life, a baby has the greatest potential to be shaped by his environment.
- Let him show you that he is unique – and that you are all he needs.

rule two

Become your own expert

'The highest activity a human being can attain is learning through understanding, because to understand is to be free.'
BENEDICT DE SPINOZA, SEVENTEENTH-CENTURY PHILOSOPHER

Know your stuff

If we are to cope with crying, we need to understand something about the subject. And to understand our babies, we might try some detective work. One obvious and important strategy is to learn your own baby's likes and dislikes – watch out for possible irritants and events that tend to bring on his tears.

In the meantime, here is a little scientific background. Because infant crying is an almost universal problem in young Western families, lots of research has been done to discover what really triggers it off. Doctors, keen to separate fact from fiction, conduct tests on real babies to find out what cheers them up and what brings them down. You may be surprised to hear some of the results . . .

- A crying baby is generally calmed by having his nappy changed, but doesn't care if the new nappy is wet or not. It is the movement and body contact he enjoys.
- Study of tube-fed babies shows that a full stomach alone does not necessarily stop the crying. Besides food, babies crave the physical sensations of sucking and being held.
- Babies cry less when they are comfortably warm.

- Babies are more likely to cry if their mothers are under stress.
- Some babies like to be swaddled closely; others dislike tight wrapping and prefer to wriggle free. But all are quieted by body contact.
- It's a myth that first-born babies cry more because of parental inexperience. Any baby in the family can be prone to crying.
- Leaving a baby to 'cry it out' without comfort often teaches him to cry for longer. Babies who receive swift tactile responses cry less overall.

One recurring theme in all these findings is the importance of body contact. Strangely, for a creature programmed for self-preservation, your baby is not particularly worried about himself. He just craves to be connected.

Did you know?

Unlike other mammals, humans are utterly dependent at birth. Primate anatomists calculate that babies actually need a twenty-one-month gestation period: nine months inside the womb and another twelve being comforted outside it. This immediately explains the baby's overwhelming need to be cuddled and soothed.

What is normal?

Parents desperately need to hear that their baby's crying is normal. So many of us struggle alone, hardly daring to share our fears, our triumphs and our tears. We just want to know we are in good company.

And we are. Studies show that the combined efforts of

American, British and Australian babies could cry us a river to rival the Mississipi. They yell frequently, they yell for hours and they yell intensively at certain times of day. Statistics like these show exactly how normal is the pattern of early crying . . .

- In Manchester, England, researchers found that six-week-old babies cried an average of forty-three minutes in twenty-four hours. (Although the range was enormous: between a mere five minutes and a massive five hours per day.) Babies who cried most at six weeks also tended to cry most later on. But by the end of the year, a quarter of all the babies cried for less than five minutes a day.
- A London study found that eight-week-old babies cried for a daily average of two hours, fifteen minutes. (Range: fifty minutes to six hours.) Babies under three months cried most often in the late afternoon and evening. There was a crying peak at two months – and another at nine months for those who cried a lot. Amazingly, 14 per cent cried for four hours or more.
- Social anthropologist Sheila Kitzinger surveyed 1,400 Australian and British families and reported a range of one to six hours' crying per day. Kitzinger suggests a relationship between constant crying and stress during pregnancy. Other researchers link crying to birth trauma.
- Ethno-paediatrician Meredith Small tells us that the average Western baby cries for twenty-two minutes a day for the first three weeks, decreasing to fourteen minutes a day by the end of three months. Babies all over the world seem to cry most in the evening.

Although crying is normal for most babies we know, this is not the whole story. On some continents, crying has not evolved to such a frenzied pitch. Babies in Africa and rural Asia, for instance, do not cry as long each day as their counterparts in North America and Europe. Here are some examples . . .

- A long-term study of Kenyan babies found they cried less than half as much as American babies.
- Research on Zincanteco babies from Mexico measured no intensive crying whatsoever.
- A comparison of Dutch, American and nomadic African babies found that although they all showed signs of crying, the American and Dutch babies cried much longer per bout and on each given day.
- Korean babies show no signs of colic, evening crying, or typical crying peaks (e.g. at two months).

Anyone who has travelled to South America, Asia or Africa will be able to confirm that – unless they are ill – babies there are rarely heard to cry. What do parents in other cultures know that we have, perhaps, forgotten? This is what we are going to explore . . .

Did you know?

The fairytale character of the 'changeling' may be based on the incessantly crying baby. In celtic belief, fey folk (fairies) stole human babies and replaced them with changelings, wizened little creatures who 'howled most piteously' and were never satisfied by nursing.

Reasons to be tearful

Some people say that babies' cries fit into a few known categories. This would be helpful if only the experts could agree which categories apply. Here is a short selection to remind you why expert lists can leave you feeling bothered, bewildered and no nearer the truth . . .

- Nanny Gina Ford names five crying categories: Hunger, Tiredness, Overtiredness, Boredom, Wind.
- Zoologist Desmond Morris suggests seven: Pain, Discomfort, Hunger, Loneliness, Over-stimulation, Under-stimulation, Frustration.
- Pat Gray, founder of the British support group Crysis, offers a more sophisticated inventory: Birth complications, Immaturity, Hunger, Colic, Low sensory threshold, Frustration and boredom, Infection and illness, Physical abnormalities, Pain or discomfort, Too much fussing, Allergies, Effects of drugs, Parental anxiety.
- The recently invented 'WhyCry' machine uses a small microphone to analyse the power and frequency of a baby's cries and sorts them into five headings: Hunger, Boredom, Discomfort, Sleepiness and Stress.
- Before we beat the batter, American psychologist Aletha J. Solter has another ingredient to throw in. She says infant crying is unlikely to be any of the above, interpreting daily tears as a necessary release of infant tension. Solter says parents must not try to suppress crying with over-feeding or jiggling the baby around. 'Probably the single, most important error made by parents,' she asserts, 'is to assume that all crying indicates an immediate need.'

So who is right? A complete list would include most of the suggestions above, because babies cry for an infinite variety of reasons, some quite simple to detect – and easily remedied – others more deep-seated and complex. A baby's cry is different with each situation and it also develops as he grows older, turning from a simple reflex to a sophisticated protest with subtle meanings and increasing emotional content.

Then there's the question of temperament. From the jungle to the desert, parents agree that some babies are more 'difficult' than others. Luckily, mothers are equipped to understand their babies' cries better than anyone else in the world. Most people can identify a child's piercing cry of pain, but studies show that mothers in particular (with their hormonal connection to the baby) can understand their babies' crying language. Even without prior baby experience, mothers make the best baby detectives.

Did you know?

Victorian and edwardian household manuals insisted that babies cried to exercise their lungs. For instance, Enquire Within Upon Everything (c. 1912) says: 'These vociferating sounds imply the effort which children make to display the strength of their lungs and exercise their organs of respiration . . .'

One extreme to the other

When a baby cries, he goes into his highest state of arousal. And so, unwittingly, does his poor mother. Tests show that from pregnancy onwards, a woman's heart races at the sound of any baby's cry, but once she gives birth, she becomes hypersensitive to her own baby. She swiftly learns what his cries might mean.

The evolved point of crying is to elicit a human response – and this, of course, is exactly what it does. The pitch and repetition of infant crying makes our nerves jangle and seeps into our bones. In years to come, there will be a similar effect when your child plays high-decibel teenage music around the house.

The upshot of all this wailing depends partly on the situation and mood of you, the baby's carer. It may depend on your upbringing, the books you read, advice from friends and family, how well supported you are – and your own feelings of self-esteem.

It also matters on which continent your baby is born (even climate can make a difference!) and *when* he arrives: is this a decade obsessed with childcare routines, or one where parents are relaxed and less controlling? Crying brings out the best and worst in people, and through early experiences, babies swiftly learn the rules of their world.

Let's consider two extremes. One tactic is to pay no heed at all. In the 1920s and 1930s, experts recommended that crying babies should be checked for serious problems, but otherwise ignored. Infants were left to cry, sometimes for hours, in their prams at the bottom of the garden. Like the no-win situation of a witch trial, babies were presumed especially mischievous if they stopped crying when mother picked them up: this, says historian Christina Hardyment, was 'a sure sign of "naughtiness."'

A friend of mine can still remember, as an older baby, lying on her back in the garden and being left to cry. She vividly recalls the branches that swayed in the canopy of trees over her head. She knew no one would come, but kept on howling anyway. She looks back on her babyhood with understandable bitterness.

Ignoring infant crying is what's known in the trade as 'counter-intuitive'. In other words, it goes against our animal instincts. While some claim that babies must be tamed, others argue that any training process should begin slowly by meeting the baby's early needs, not thwarting them.

And so, at the other extreme, we have the 'in-arms' methods, where parents carry their babies around in slings or in their arms, sleeping near them at night, responding instantly to signs of hunger or pain. Frequent or constant carrying has been practised for thousands of years and is still the world's most popular form of babycare. It's a pre-emptive strike that offers maximum comfort before baby has the chance even to think about turning up the volume.

It might reassure you to picture these two very different approaches – 'avoidance' versus 'total contact' – and to imagine how many ways there must be to deal with a crying baby. Between these radical tactics there is an infinite number of approaches, many of which might work for you.

The more contact you can offer your baby, the more satisfying the long-term results will be.

Did you know?

The relationship between a Japanese mother and her baby is traditionally so close that anthropologists have called it 'skinship'. Young Japanese mothers tend to use modern front slings, but the classic way is to bind baby to the mother's back.

Take that call

A baby's cry is often compared to an alarm signal, but alarms make me want to run away, flapping my arms unhelpfully (and then where would my baby be?). So let's try a less distressing metaphor – imagine the crying as the ring tone on a mobile telephone. It's just a question of trying to find the button with the icon of a little green receiver on it. Don't be afraid to pick up.

'If only babycare were that simple,' you say. 'If my baby is a mobile phone, why did Nature equip him with such an annoying ring tone? A newborn baby has an unbelievably immature brain and is utterly helpless and dependent on his carers,' (you add), 'yet his only mode of communication is a yell that penetrates two doors and a turned-up telly. Constant crying doesn't bring me running, it makes me want to escape. Perhaps Mother Nature would like to explain herself and her two-bit telephone system, because it's spoiling all the fun.'

We all know that listening to a baby cry for hours is a form of torture, and some babies *are* capable of yelling for hours. Full-blown screaming swiftly alienates the very people who are supposed to take care of the baby. When we think of those poor parents who endure four or more hours' crying a day, it does look as though Nature's system is badly designed.

However, we must also wonder why the call-and-response system worked so well for many thousands of years. Only the most recent childcare philosophies, dating from around the 1920s, advocate letting the baby 'call' without getting a real 'response'. Popular today is a modified version of this, known as Controlled Crying. It usually involves leaving the baby to 'cry it out' for a pre-set number of minutes without picking up. The aim is to teach the baby that crying will not get him anywhere.

Unfortunately, stringent methods can teach a baby one or two things besides submission. They can teach him that he's only acceptable when he is 'good' and that 'good' means passive. They can teach him that it's simply not worth trying to communicate his needs – a syndrome known as 'learned helplessness'. They may teach him that the world is a hostile place in which he is not entirely welcome. And they may even lead him into self-harming habits, such as head-banging and incessant rocking.

Of course babycare really isn't as simple as taking a telephone call. Your telephone does not ring louder and more insistently if you ignore it. The sound of your telephone may send your pulse racing, but it rarely fills you with feelings of panic or despair. Nor does your telephone suddenly stop crying and flash you the most wonderful smile. No metaphor is quite like the experience of caring for a real, live baby.

But there is overwhelming evidence, from hundreds of different cultures, that babies who are picked up and carried a lot cry less than babies whose cries are ignored.

To help us find practical ways of applying age-old ideas that work, we shall journey across centuries and continents, to places where the original babycare communication system is still in operation. The future lies not merely in following our own society's trends, but of opening our hearts and minds to a range of ideas.

We need to understand why crying can sometimes be a good thing; why the support of a caring community is important for anyone in charge of a baby; the real facts about colic and the importance of massage, lullabies, tactile nursing and co-sleeping. We will find out how to encompass a baby's cries, deal with depression and make the most of the good days. Because there will be good days, I promise.

Did you know?

Anthropologists observing nomadic !kung San women of the Kalahari desert notice that they soothe their babies' cries within seconds. Mothers instinctively played their part in the ancient call-and-response system and no attempt is made to teach a newborn baby the principles of delayed gratification.

Rule Two in a nutshell

- Become your own expert. Arm yourself with the facts about crying and you will find it easier to feel sympathetic with your baby.
- Infant crying is quite normal, but we can learn useful lessons from those cultures where babies are never left to cry.
- There are thousands of theories why babies cry: but a parent's intuition is the best gauge of all.
- Many cultures use close contact to reduce crying to the bare minimum. For decades, Western culture has experimented with reduced or minimal contact to try to achieve the same effect.
- At the two extremes, we might ignore the baby's crying or carry him around everywhere. Somewhere along the scale, there will be solutions which will work for you.

rule three

Let your baby get a word in edgeways

Rachel rocks baby Emma, who is crying incessantly.

MONICA: 'Try feeding her again.'

RACHEL: 'I already fed her.'

MONICA (impatiently): 'I know, that's why I said "again".'

PHOEBE: ' Right, you guys, we can't turn on each other, OK? (points accusingly at baby). That's just what she wants!'

FRIENDS, 'THE ONE WHERE EMMA CRIES'
TV SERIES 9 (NBC, USA 2002)

Babies love routine – it's schedules they don't appreciate

We must never forget that babies thrive on an excessive amount of love. Love is the only routine they need: the routine care of an affectionate human being to hold them and embrace their fears. In shorthand, this is 'close-contact nurture'. It doesn't spoil babies, it fills them with the strength they will one day need to be independent.

Babies can't get enough attention. But busy twenty-first century parents must decide how much they are willing to give. New mothers and fathers, bewildered by the inevitable choice of childcare options, may be persuaded to opt for those which are most concrete and dogmatic. Some approaches are as strict as a calorie-controlled diet, with lists of Dos and Don't and minutely detailed descriptions of where to be when and what to do next. They tend to promise a heaven where your baby will sleep deeply, cry seldom and be no bother at all.

But expecting a baby to sleep, feed and play by the clock is like expecting the trains to run on time. Timetables devised by experts can cause unnecessary stress and are often in themselves a recipe for failure. Ever since the recent trend for schedule-based books, breastfeeding counsellors and post-natal teachers have reported an increasing number of crisis calls from mothers whose babies won't play ball.

Our new-found fondness for timetables is understandable in a world where so many conflicting theories collide. But I know I could never devise a routine to suit every desperate reader, every hapless baby in the land. The best routines are those which are flexible and evolve from experience. They are the outcome of a real-live relationship with a real-live child.

One of the first jobs of the new parent is to get to know his or her own baby. This becomes almost impossible if your life is dominated by rules and you find you keep looking at the clock before responding to your baby's cries. Don't let any book or method come between you and your child. That essential, early relationship should be a time of trial and error, mix-ups and making up. This is your honeymoon and you can take all the time in the world.

Did you know?

The idea of regulating a baby's life by the clock dates back to the late nineteenth-century and advice like this from victorian author Dr Pye Henry Chavasse: 'A mother ought to suckle her baby at stated times. It is a bad habit to give him the bosom every time he cries, regardless of the cause . . .' Why not try ignoring the clocks for a day? This is how babycare is still practised in most countries today.

Babies will be babies

Instead of living in the present with their babies, many parents are preoccupied by the future. They fear that if the baby is nursed on demand, carried everywhere, cuddled at night, they will never be able to move him on from these 'habits'. But, of course, they will. When it comes to child-care, it is important to live for today. Don't be afraid to start what you think you can't finish!

Remember you're the grown-up – you can change tack whenever you want. Early babyhood demands an intense kind of parenting that the older child simply wouldn't appreciate. We put babies in nappies without worrying that they'll still need them at twenty-five. We feed them on fruit purées knowing that they'll soon progress to solid meals.

The more security you offer a small baby, the more secure he becomes. The formula is simple – and it works. Later, there will be time for letting go, for weaning towards in-dependence, for introducing discipline and responsibility. But a baby should be allowed to be a baby.

Some days, your baby will want to nurse more – that's OK. Some days he may sleep less – that's fine, too. Nowhere in this rulebook will you find a prescription for your baby's behaviour. Babies don't need prescriptions because they are perfectly able to self-regulate. How much simpler it is to act on this belief than to go through early years of anxiety and mistrust.

I was once asked by a young newspaper reporter how babies learn to fall asleep. I had to explain that babies don't need to learn this skill – they fall asleep by themselves while in the womb and continue to do so after birth. She was genuinely amazed by such an idea. And yet it is a common misconception that babies must be 'taught' to sleep. Some-times, we really get babies' needs upside down. It's not sleep that babies object to, it's being left alone while they do it.

It's a similar story with breastfeeding. Some health professionals have a dislike for demand-nursing, yet the most successful breastfeeding in the world takes place in cultures that put no limits on the frequency or length of feeds. Most babies like to suckle little and often.* Equipped with a baggy jumper and an open mind, a mother can feed her baby anywhere and people around her cannot even see what's going on.

Let's think about babies in Asia, Africa and South America – the ones who are rarely heard to cry. They are no different from our babies – they didn't know which continent they were going to land in. The main difference in their lives is that their parents are not cynical about their infantile needs. They simply let them be babies, indulging them for the first few months, even years, trusting absolutely that they will, one day, stop being so needy. Much held, their babies have very little to cry for.

Babies think they are at the centre of the universe. We know differently, of course, but I believe they should be granted their post-natal fantasy. Why shouldn't tiny humans be allowed to wallow in pleasure-seeking, self-centred, ego-forming delight? It's true that babies can seem sponge-like in their ability to soak up every ounce of energy you've got. But we must never forget the cycle of pleasure to be gained in giving. And I do believe that society's desire to raise happy, independent children is best served by enjoying and indulging babies while they are small.

We need to trust in our babies at every stage in their development. They all grow up in the end.

*Bottle-fed babies have a different pattern. They tend to feed less frequently and more regularly, but still appreciate tender cuddles and lots of physical contact.

Did you know?

Human infants, like baby monkeys, are programmed
to respond to their carers in three overlapping stages:
1) using their early reflexes; 2) showing affectionate
attachment (smiling, gurgling, etc.); 3) seeking security
(running for comfort and protection). Finally, they
reach independence. According to social scientist
Ashley Montagu, 'the most important of the young
animal's experiences, for its subsequent development,
is bodily contact with its mother . . .'

You got rhythm

Don't try to be your baby's boss – it's too much like hard
work. Sure, you're in charge really, but babycare should be
a dance, a dialogue, a discussion – not a dictation. Why ruin
those precious early months by introducing the atmosphere
of a highly organized office?

The key to enjoying a baby is to fall into rhythm with
him. At the same time, he can't help falling into rhythm
with you. The quickest way to find yourself out of synch
with your baby is to impose feeds when he's not hungry,
sleep when he doesn't need it, and conversation when he's
not in the mood. And yet this is precisely the struggle that
many schedules create.

You may feel you want to take control after your baby
is born. You'd like more sleep, it would be good to get
dressed before midday, leave the house and even socialize
occasionally . . . sometimes it seems as though you'll never
live a normal life again. But all these things *are* possible,
even though you may be putting your baby's needs on high
priority.

Paradoxically, the schedule-following parent can become a slave to her own timetable. She cannot leave the house when it is time for the baby's nap. She must feed her baby when directed and endure his hunger cries until then. According to some authors, she even has set times for expressing milk, or doing her laundry. Her life may have a certain predictability, but it is also seriously limiting and unresponsive to her own needs.

There is another way. By keeping baby close to you – in physical contact as much as you are able – it is possible to carry on with your own life to a large extent. A much-held baby becomes increasingly passive and easy to carry. He takes naps when he needs them. He suckles when he feels like it. He cries much less. You don't have to train him, or worry about whether or not you are doing the 'right thing'. Before long, and without any struggles, your baby starts to fall into the rhythms that you create.

Your baby can be in heaven without your life becoming hell.

Did you know?

When asked by researchers how often they breastfed their babies, Egyptian mothers simply had no idea. It did not occur to them to clock-watch their way through their baby's day. The obedient Gina Ford follower, by contrast, will know at what time she opened her baby's curtains (9.45 a.m.), at what time she expressed '2 oz from the second breast' (10.30 a.m.) and at what time she allowed her baby a 'good kick' (5.45 p.m.).

Is anybody listening?

It used to be fashionable to suggest that crying was good for babies. But theories about lungs and exercise do not take into account the stress hormones that babies release, the chronic stiffening of frustrated limbs as they flail about for comfort, or the negative effects of programming a child to cry for his every want.

Babies are not built for hours of daily crying. It means the call-and-response system has broken down and they are on full alert for catastrophe. A screaming baby is one of Nature's most alarming sounds and it is astonishing that so many Western parents quickly learn how to tolerate or ignore it. (Of course, we are educated to do this over years of observing other parents and hearing their philosophies. Childcare ideas are highly contagious.)

Since Mother Nature didn't intend babies to do all this wailing, she put in lots of pre-crying stages, giving us the chance to notice and act before things get desperate:

1. Baby starts to wriggle and fidget.
2. He makes grunting noises, turns his head, looks uncomfortable.
3. He kicks out with his feet, becomes visibly agitated.
4. His face wrinkles and the first, soft, whimper begins. There may be tears.
5. He begins to cry, at a louder volume.
6. Untended, the crying becomes rhythmical, repetitive. Crying becomes harder to soothe.
7. Prolonged crying sets into a rhythmical pattern ('la, la' or 'wa, wa').
8. Baby's legs retract as if in pain; his face may become outraged and red.

9. Emergency mode: the baby screams as if his life were in danger.

When parents are allowed to respond to their babies with intuition and feeling (rather than responding to schedules or timetables with feeling!), the baby's distress is usually soothed by stage four. If the baby is being held or worn on a sling, crying can be anticipated as early as stage one.

Stage nine is not designed for everyday use. Yet this level of screaming is usual for many babies, especially those undergoing systems of infant training. When they are upset, they move straight into full-blown crying, as they have learnt that their early signals are being ignored.

If only we would let our babies get a word in edgeways. They deserve to be heard.

Did you know?

Researchers estimate that the average baby experiences 4,000 crying sessions in the first two years of life. Of course, his caregivers experience the 4,000 sessions, too.

Learning to cry

Mothers in other cultures simply do not understand why we let babies cry. They certainly don't understand why experts write books on *how* to leave babies to cry! Women of the Sioux tribe in Dakota, for instance, say that white parents 'teach their children to cry'. Sioux grandparents complain at the American hospital practice of separating mother and baby at birth, because it teaches the usually passive Sioux baby to 'cry like a white baby'.

In Kenya, mothers of the Gusii tribe do not let their

babies cry for any reason. Their aim is to create quiet, co-operative children, and all their babycare tactics are designed for peace. Babies are carried at all times and their needs met before each wriggle has turned to a whimper.

When shown a video of an American mother changing the diaper of her screaming baby, Gusii mothers became extremely upset. They were amazed that neither the baby's mother nor his grandmother was able to soothe the crying immediately. But in fact, the American baby was not used to being quickly soothed. He had learnt to by-pass the early signals of his discomfort and move straight on to ferocious wailing.

Babies whose needs are swiftly met take longer to move from subtle signals to full-blown crying. Amazingly, this means they are learning to postpone their demands. It is a paradox that could save your life: respond quickly and your baby will learn to be more patient. Subtly, slowly, but ever so surely, he is moving towards maturity.

Did you know?

Many cultures have fearful taboos about leaving a baby to cry. Jamaican tradition says that if a baby is left crying by himself, the duppies, or ghosts, will take him away.

You *will* leave the apartment

Some prospective parents know it all. I certainly had it sussed before the children came along. The key thing (I had read in a reputable women's magazine) was not to keep any poisonous plants in the garden. I was very proud of this information, which happened to be the sum total of my knowledge about childcare. I might have had a university degree and a fondness for babies, but I obviously knew nothing about the task ahead.

This and other vague ideas – like working from home with the baby sleeping sweetly in a Moses basket at my feet – were soon scotched when it transpired that most of my brain cells had liquefied during pregnancy and the rest were fried to a sizzle during the birth. I couldn't so much as read a magazine, let alone write an article, which was something of a handicap for a writer.

When I was breastfeeding (and I always seemed to be breastfeeding), I used to sit for hours, just nursing and watching the dust gather on the living-room furniture. I had bought a snazzy pushchair which weighed a ton and took three skilled labourers to erect, so I didn't go out much. I had yet to discover the joys of the baby sling. What use was my insider knowledge on poisonous plants, when I couldn't even move to open the back door?

Yet I began to learn that sitting around, waiting and watching were worthwhile things to do, as they gave me the chance to relax. Many years later, now I know that even fully grown children still take up a vast amount of a mother's time and energies, I look back on those early days as a kind of preparation for parenthood. Pinned to the sofa, with a baby on the breast and a glass of water beside me to quench my unending thirst, I had time to adjust to my astonishing new role. I had, after all, become a mother.

But when she cried – oh, when my first baby cried! – my inner calm deserted me. My heartbeat raced, I felt feverish with despair, I didn't know what to do. My best friend Frédérique, who had two children already and a very capable air, could take Frances and soothe her within seconds. I felt useless. I wanted to capture Fred's technique and bottle it. I wanted to be her. I felt like Rachel, the character in *Friends*, who spent a whole episode trying to pacify her new baby, Emma, until finally, friend Monica took over:

> *Rachel: 'Oh God, what am I gonna do, you guys? I can't even comfort my own baby. I'm the worst mother ever!'*
> *(. . . Monica calms the baby)*
> *Rachel: 'Oh my God, you got her to stop crying!'*
> *Monica: (pleased) 'Yes I did!'*
> *Rachel: 'You are the official Baby Crier Stopper! You're never leaving the apartment!'*
> *Monica: (stunned) 'Say what?'*

Since Emma was a fictional baby and this was a sitcom, everyone did eventually manage to leave the apartment and continue with their riotous sitcom lives. But even without the magic of television, there is a life waiting for you beyond the crying-room walls. The next Rule allows us to consider techniques for coping with a crying baby and for easing any feelings of desperation and dread. It's time to tackle the tears.

Did you know?

A crying baby triggers a wide range of emotions in his mother and other carers. After initial feelings of agitation, these may include resentment, frustration, anger and guilt, exhaustion, depression and even hormone imbalance! No wonder crying is frequently a cause of household crisis.

Rule Three in a nutshell

- The best routines evolve from the conversation between yourself and your baby. No schedule written by a stranger could possibly meet all your needs and is likely to create unnecessary tensions.
- When we let them get a word in edgeways, we see that babies are able to communicate with subtle signs.
- Carrying babies around and responding quickly to their demands – surprisingly – teaches them to defer those demands.
- Learn to surrender to your astonishing new role. Give yourself time to get into parenthood and recognize the string of emotions triggered by your crying baby. One day, you will be able to leave the apartment . . .

rule four

Hold the tears

'When love and skill work together, expect a masterpiece.'
JOHN RUSKIN, NINETEENTH-CENTURY THINKER

Read the signs

We have seen how crying begins with small twitches and movements, tiny indications of a baby's discomfort. But babies' pre-crying signals are even more subtle and sophisticated than this. If we look closely, we can sometimes see them making the primitive, reflexive gestures which hint at *why* they are crying.

1. **Your baby passes the back of his hand over his mouth. He opens his mouth to one side and begins to 'root'** . . . Your baby would like to feed/comfort-suckle. Rooting is a nipple-seeking reflex, where the baby turns his head to one side, opening his mouth wide. It is a necessary preparation for feeding, as he has to take a large area of the areola (the area around the nipple) into his mouth to milk the breast effectively. A baby has a deep need to suckle and, if you are happy to let him feed quite often, it is best not to worry too much about whether he is really hungry. Left to their own devices, babies suckle on and off, day and night, and in most cultures are allowed to do so.
2. **Your baby rubs his eyes, fidgets and yawns. His eyelids look heavy** . . . Of course, he is ready for sleep!
3. **Your baby ignores you when you try to play with him.**

He even turns his head away . . . He doesn't want to be stimulated now. If you insist, he may become agitated.

4. **Your baby's knees draw up as if in pain. His cries are piercing and rhythmical. He goes red in the face . . .** These sound like the symptoms of stomach pain or indigestion, often associated with colic.

All these gestures (and others, which may be unique to your own baby) are an essential part of the baby's struggle to make himself heard. But minute signals are easily overlooked unless we keep our babies close to us and get to know their smallest movements well. If you carry your baby around with you, in your arms or on a sling, the two of you will learn to communicate through body-sensing.

An extreme example of this is the way that mothers in many cultures anticipate their babies' toilet needs. In the thousands of years before nappies, mothers would hold their babies out for toileting. In the Canadian Arctic, a Netsilik mother traditionally carries her baby inside her fur parka and whips him out just in time. In African countries, women hold their babies out in the bushes.

When curious anthropologists asked Ugandan mothers how they knew when to do this, the mothers responded with an incredulous question: 'How do *you* know when *you* have to go?' As far as they knew, all mothers had this level of intimacy and understanding with their babies. Scientists have since discovered that, when the baby is jammed against your body, you can feel his involuntary thigh spasms as soon as his bladder is full. It is this sensation which enables the African and other mothers to respond so swiftly.

No wonder the sling-held baby cries less than the baby in a cot, push-chair or car seat. His carers are almost constantly in touch with his ever-communicating body.

Did you know?

An American study found that a little more baby-carrying results in a lot less crying. Babies carried 4.4 hours per day cried 43 per cent less than babies carried for 2.7 hours – a difference of only 1.7 hours' carrying!

Simple solutions

Sometimes a little swaying is all it takes to make baby subside into seamless sleep or regain his calm. Sometimes an energetic jog around the block is required to release the pent-up tensions of the day.

Ordinary crying requires simple remedies and parents swiftly learn what works with their own child. My only thought would be: do not deny the baby his apparent needs for comfort or food. When he is small, his needs and wants are the same thing. He is not trying to trick you, or 'wrap you around his little finger'.

- If it's hunger – let him feed.
- If it's sleep – let him fall asleep on your body, or near you. Wrapped next to you with a cloth or sling, he will fall asleep as easily as he did in the womb. If your baby needs help to calm down, hold him in the dark. Lie down with him, or gently sway. Offer minimal stimulation. Most babies like to suckle themselves to sleep. Sucking centres the baby and soothes his whole body. (You don't have to imprison yourself in the bedroom. You might, for instance, have the television on quietly or read a book.) Softly sing a lullaby.
- If it's boredom or minor agitation – try distracting him with touch, eye-to-eye contact and soft words.

- If it's pent-up energy – rock your baby more vigorously, dance or jog with him.
- If he's beside himself and you've been indoors for more than two hours – wrap him in a sling and go for a brisk walk. A lot of crying is simply a plea for fresh air. Evening crying is often the result of tensions built up during the day. It's a good time to head outdoors.

Did you know?

The most common single remedy for soothing baby's tears around the world is nursing: researchers in Africa, Japan, India and South America all found that a baby was likely to be put to the breast within seconds of starting to cry.

We will rock you

'You know you're a second-time new mother if you find yourself jiggling the baby up and down vigorously when it is the toddler that is crying.'
Philippa Need, New Generation,
magazine of the UK's National Childbirth Trust

The way you move with your baby will depend on many factors: the way you use your own body, for instance, your baby's crying patterns, the way you feel inside. No one can prescribe these things. Rocking a baby is an instinctive act – studies show that parents automatically rock their babies at between sixty and seventy moves a minute, approximately the rate of the beating heart. This is not a skill we need to be taught.

When you think about it, it's obvious why babies love to be swung gently from side to side. They have spent nine months in the swell of the womb. Like passengers alighting from a cruise ship, they feel a little lost on dry land. For years to come, they will seek out the comfort of rocking, whether in the security of a parent's arms or the motion of a swing. If left for long enough alone in a motionless cot, they will start to rock themselves, in a rhythmical, comfort-seeking motion.

Embracing a baby while rocking is good for him. It increases his heart rate and stimulates his circulation. It helps improve muscle tone (essential for babies, who cannot take exercise for themselves) and promotes healthy breathing. It even stimulates and improves your baby's digestion, helping premature infants to gain weight. No wonder babies find comfort in this, the simplest of parent-craft remedies.

Did you know?

Nature did not originally intend us to spend hours simply rocking and jiggling our babies about. This ritual is a substitute for an earlier, more active human lifestyle when, hunting and gathering for food, parents and older siblings would keep babies strapped to their backs all day. Babies evolved to be little nomads, and all they want is to come along for the ride.

Surround sound

Besides movement, there is another basic human tool for calming cranky babies. Again, if we think of conditions in the womb, we realize that babies have been listening to months of reassuring swishing, distant lulling (of their mother's voice) and the regular rhythm of the maternal heartbeat. When we surround our newborns with similar sounds, they immediately become more composed.

Even childcare authors who advocate leaving a baby alone to cry recognize the benefits of soothing sounds. They may suggest that parents use the hours of crying to do the vacuuming, which has the dual effect of soothing the baby and blocking out the screaming. In fact, the level of noise in the womb can be almost deafening – during labour it has been measured to between eighty and ninety decibels, which is actually louder than the vacuum cleaner!

Consider how peculiarly quiet the world must be to a baby arriving home from hospital (unless he lives with his extended family, in a community, or has a ready-made clan of brothers and sisters). For a first baby, the sudden change to an empty house must in itself be unsettling. And to think how much time new parents spend tiptoeing around their new babies . . . What babies need is not silence, nor sudden noise, but the reassurance of hubbub – a context for life.

Research on cot death tells us that human background noise (combined with lots of touch and movement) helps to stimulate the baby into regular sleeping and breathing patterns. Nursery product manufacturers have also cottoned on to the idea that babies benefit from surround sound. There are many tapes you can buy, offering babies a diet of white noise, heartbeat simulations, lullabies or snatches of music by Mozart – to improve the infant brain.

Sounds certainly pacify, but they do so best when they are coupled with the reassurance of touch. If you are prepared to hold your baby and experiment with your own voice, you will be able to create a hypnotic environment which your baby may be unable to resist. Here are two really simple ideas . . .

- Try shushing your baby's tears away. Mothers around the world shush their babies to soothe and keep them quiet. They purse their lips just a few inches from the baby's ear and begin a steady shushing. (Just that – the sound 'Shshshsh.') American paediatrician Dr Harvey Karp says the shushing should increase in volume and stay quite loud until the baby's crying subsides.

- Learn one or two easy lullabies to sing to your baby. Sad to report, our repertoire of lullabies has diminished over the last few generations. More and more mothers claim they have 'forgotten the words', or lack the confidence to sing. But babies are not perfectionists. They just long to be lulled into a state of peace and calm. The only essential part of the lullaby is the 'lull', a kind of mantra that is used by almost every culture to pacify its babies. New lullabies are easily created, using simple speech patterns and sympathetic tunes. See Rule Eight: *Songs That Soothe*.

See what musical magic you can weave.

Did you know?

Humans like to dance to music that mimics the sounds of the womb. Unborn babies can hear their mother's steady heartbeat as well as that of their own heart, which beats at around twice the speed. Rhythms in 6/8 – typical dance music, like the song 'I could have danced all night' – mimic this pattern, making us want to sway, or rock, from side to side. All over the world, people love to dance with their babies and the babies adore to dance.

It's ok to cry

Some developmental psychologists believe that one third of infant crying is unrelated to any cause. They say crying is a release for babies' stored hurts, perhaps from birth trauma, over-stimulation or physical pains from the past. They talk of a baby's *need* to cry and say we shouldn't suppress it. But nor do they suggest that parents leave a baby alone to scream.

It would be wonderful if we could look into a baby's eyes and see – as parents from other cultures believe they can – into his soul. Even with this belief, any theories on a baby's hidden feelings will always remain speculation. What we can learn from this approach, however, is an acceptance of crying and a really important technique on how to cope with it.

Most soothing methods assume – understandably – that we want the bawling to stop. Leaving baby to cry alone in a cot makes this assumption, even though the child may cry for hours before he 'learns' that no one is listening. Parents are told to harden their hearts against his tears. Turn up the telly, do the vacuuming . . . what you can't hear won't unhinge you.

Close-contact soothing also assumes that we want the crying to go away. As we have seen, this may involve distracting, nursing or rocking the baby. But what happens when the crying won't stop? What do you do then? Is it time to put him down, walk away and leave him to his own devices?

Or should the jiggling just get more fast and furious? Some parents say their babies won't fall asleep unless they are danced energetically around every night. This may be good for post-natal weight loss, but if you find your bedtime routine exhausting, you need another approach.

Babies rarely need us to act like personal trainers in order to unwind.

If we can't hand the baby over to someone else and we want to go on comforting, then we need to learn to *encompass* his tears. We need to relax.

Did you know?

It is not necessary to know what a baby is crying about in order to help him. Developmental psychologist Aletha Jauch Solter says, 'trust the baby to do what he needs to do . . . pay attention to him without trying to stop him or distract him.'

You are the still waters

Learn to encircle your baby as he cries. Find the still-point within yourself so you can hold him without feelings of guilt, agitation or fear. Caress, don't suppress.

'Encompassing' is the word I use for empathizing with a crying baby. It is a skill I developed over years of soothing my own babies – particularly Joe, my third, who cried more than the others in the first three months of his life. My early pregnancy with him had been stressful for me and somehow it felt appropriate that he should have something to get off his chest. I wanted to let him cry it out, but not on his own. I wanted to be there for him.

So after a certain amount of swaying, rocking, stroking and bouncing Joe around, I would just flop into a chair and let him rest heavy against my body. I might hold him loosely in my arms. Instead of becoming increasingly frantic (as undoubtedly happened when I held Frances, my first baby), I worked on unwinding my own body and mind. I learnt how to detach myself very slightly, so that the feelings I had were sympathetic, not overwhelming. Instead of trying to stop Joe's screaming, I would work on untightening my stiffening muscles.

At first, it was hard to encompass Joe's crying, as I am highly susceptible to the emotions aroused by a distressed and screaming baby. I could feel myself going hot and cold under the tearful tension of his little body. But there was no point in both of us being worked up to fever pitch. One of us simply had to chill out and gradually I learnt how. The sooner I could calm down, the sooner he found his own peace.

A crying baby may be in a state of panic, but he needs his carers to stay serene. We need to learn how to encompass the crying and become the baby's comfort zone without getting too stressed ourselves. And the best way to achieve this is to introduce this thought:

Don't try to make the crying stop.

As soon as you release yourself from the burden of trying to end the crying, you find yourself at one with your baby. It can be a wonderful release. Perhaps for the first time, you are able to accept him as he is – a tiny, vulnerable creature who cannot help his tears. Gone are all the judgments, the feelings of guilt, the looking for causes, the justifications, the attempts to get everything right, the resentment, the soul-searching. Your baby is crying. You know it, you're not running away, but there's nothing more you can do. So long as you are sure he is not ill, or hungry, or in pain, you are prepared to sit this one out.

And sooner than you think, you may find the tears subside.

Did you know?

Visualization helps you to encompass
your child's crying effectively. Try this . . .

*I let my baby bathe in my embrace. I am the still
waters. I let her agitation flow through me and beyond
me. I can help to absorb the shock of new life. I have
the power to comfort my baby, but I do not have to
share in her distress.*

Rule Four in a nutshell

- Every baby has a repertoire of signals just waiting
  for you to detect. The earlier you respond to these
  signs, the more swiftly the baby will be soothed.
- Babies' most usual reasons for crying are also most
  easily remedied.
- Let your responses be natural – use your body to
  move with your baby's rhythms; your voice to lull
  him into tranquillity.
- If, after all the obvious measures, your baby still
  needs to cry, do not try to stop him.
- Learn to encompass the crying and your baby may
  find he has nothing to fight after all. You are both on
  the same side and he knows he really is welcome in
  the world.

rule five

Turn up the heat

Colic drops

We never imagine it will happen to us. The nightmare of a baby who won't stop crying is something pregnant couples prefer not to contemplate and new parents hate to admit. But surveys tells us that around 15 per cent of babies in Western culture refuse to be soothed by ordinary means.

Swaying, hushing and singing are not enough for the colicky baby. Evening after evening, for hours on end, he fusses and frets, or emits ear-piercing shrieks. It makes no difference how much you rock or jig him around. It's like the house alarm going off when you're trapped inside and have forgotten the combination, and it's enough to drive anyone crazy.

But what is colic, really? Because it is defined by a bundle of symptoms – and these are a matter for debate – some doctors claim there is no such thing. In all events, 'colic' is not a disease, but a description of that excessive, unsoothable crying which so many babies under three months display.

Health professionals say 90 per cent of cases are misdiagnosed. A strict medical definition goes by the 'rule of threes': i.e. the baby cries for more than three hours a day on more than three days a week. Yet one half of the babies brought to crying clinics do not cry this much. And although first-time parents are more likely to seek help, first-time babies are no more likely to be colicky than their siblings.

Acoustic tests suggest that the colic cry has specific qualities: it is higher pitched, more jittery, rhythmic and intense than other infant crying. The baby's face becomes scarlet and scrunched in anguish and his mouth appears square at the corners. Typically, his back will arch and his legs draw up as if in pain. Or he may simply fret for hours. His distress is prolonged, unpredictable and – unlike other types of crying – inconsolable.

In studies, mothers were delighted to find that experienced midwives were no better at soothing their colicky babies than they were themselves. Research shows that the parents of crying babies are just as competent as other parents. It's not a question of lack of ability, but of babies who defy their parents' best efforts.

Nor is colic a condition of modern life. Bouts of colic affect breastfed babies just as much as those on formula milks. Babies in other cultures suffer from colic, too. In Kenya, for instance, Gusii babies get a condition called Enyancha (The Lake) in which their genitals are supposedly disturbed by the wind moving off Lake Victoria. The 'cure' for Enyancha is the same as colic cures the world over: strap baby into a sling and bounce him around.

Although bouncing baby is a natural response, research suggests that jiggling and carrying rarely relieve the symptoms of babies already labelled as 'colicky'. This simple fact may give us a clue to the condition. Perhaps it is a vicious circle – a habit learnt in the first few weeks by the sensitive baby and not easily broken. Perhaps the answer lies in not waiting until colic becomes established before we offer our babies what scientists call 'proximal care' – i.e. carrying them around a lot from birth. Perhaps this is why colic is less usual in cultures where babies are routinely carried on the body, frequently fed and soothed from the start. These parents go for prevention rather than cure.

One thing, at any rate, is certain. Colic usually disappears by the baby's fourth month. It's a newborn phenomenon and older babies simply seem to grow out of it.

Did you know?

American campaigners trying to raise awareness of the dangers of shaking a crying baby have coined a new term for colic: 'the period of purple crying'. Purple is an acronym for the characteristics of the condition:

peak pattern
unpredictable
resistant to soothing
pain-like face
long bouts
evening cry

The aim is to reassure parents that this type of crying is extremely common in babies under three months.

Crying and the ill baby

The word colic comes from the Greek *kōlikos*, which refers to the colon. Generations of parents remain convinced their colicky babies experience some kind of digestive pain. Yet colic rarely has an identifiable physical cause – if it does, it stops being called colic and transforms into something official, like 'gastro-oesophageal reflux' (where the baby cries from the sensation of food and acid returning from the stomach).

Nevertheless, if you think you have a colicky baby, it is important to get his symptoms checked out. When a baby cries excessively, your doctor will want to make sure he is not ill, whether from a short-term virus or a chronic condition. Most inconsolable babies find themselves sooner or later in the doctor's surgery, undergoing checks and tests to eliminate possible problems.

Frequent crying can be triggered off by many different conditions and it would be unhelpful to list them all here. Some babies experience intense crying bouts after vaccination; others react to something in their own or their mothers' diet. Bottle-fed babies who cry a lot are likely to have their formula milk changed by anxious parents, yet only 1–2 per cent of babies in general (10 per cent of colicky babies) actually have a cow's milk intolerance. Scientists point out that babies often mature out of colic at just the time when parents feel they have got the milk right. Once again, it is hard to prove cause and effect.

However, crying is rarely the problem with very ill babies. Crying takes a great deal of strength and seriously unwell babies have little energy to spare. They cry weakly or not at all. The sickly-looking, passive, unprotesting baby is a worry to anyone who cares for him. His appearance even makes a difference to the way he is handled: studies show that very ill babies are touched and stimulated less than well babies. On top of this, health concerns make parents feel more guilty or inadequate to the task ahead.

Whether or not your ill baby cries, don't keep him at arm's length. Unless he cannot be handled for some reason, this is a good time to get truly in touch.

Among the Gusii women of Kenya, it is traditional for the ill baby to be given intensive physical and spiritual protection for up to six weeks after his birth. The baby remains constantly in his mother's arms, close to the cooking fire, even if it is hot outside. Fathers also have rituals to perform which help to bind the magic that will keep the baby safe from harm. A pair of enveloping arms tell the ill baby that his pain is understood.

Did you know?

A baby's cry of pain is easy to recognize. It starts with a sharp intake of breath and a sudden yell. The first cry is long and the baby holds his breath between outbursts.

Too much, too young

Premature babies have their own pattern of tears. At birth, when they are often ill and dependent on machinery, they may be passive and less likely to protest. But after a few weeks, premature babies tend to cry more than average and their cry is at a higher, more irritating pitch. Parents may find this particularly stressful, especially since it is harder to engage the premature baby in positive ways.

Studies show that preemies tend to be more irritable, quicker to cry, easier to over-stimulate and harder to soothe than their mature counterparts. And – which is tough on new parents – the premature baby is unlikely to smile until six to eight weeks after his due date, a significant delay in the joy of early interaction. All these factors contribute to the statistic that premature babies are at an increased risk of abuse or neglect.

Small-for-dates babies often go through intrusive therapies to help them survive. And doctors are aware that the very treatments which save their lives also increase their distress. Respirators can damage lungs, eyes and ears and the typical preemie has to endure up to four blood tests a day. These two-minute heel-lancing procedures obviously cause the babies pain – in studies, they all wriggle and cry – and their heart rates reach critical levels. Life outside the womb is hard work for the underdeveloped baby.

We have already seen how 'kangaroo care' – placing the premature infant skin-to-skin on his parent's chest – helps to restore his health and boost the confidence of his shell-shocked parents. In fact, there are many examples of folk treatments designed to soothe the baby who has been born too soon . . .

- In Ghana, the early baby is protected 'like an egg'. He lies, unwashed, in his mother's arms for at least seven days.
- In the frozen north, tiny Inuit babies are wrapped in the soft skin of a seabird and hung over an oil lamp for warmth. After that, they are carried everywhere inside their mother's parka.
- In Mozambique, the tiny baby is wrapped in a kanga (the African woman's wrap) to keep warm against her body. If he is too weak to suckle, he is given expressed breast-milk with a spoon.

Your premature baby may seem delicate or frail; he may even be connected to life-saving equipment, but he will surely benefit from some remedial skin-to-skin contact to ease the trauma of those early months. This is a lesson that hospitals have been steadily learning over the past forty years. Most now promote the philosophy that premature babies thrive best with the stimulation of loving touch.

Did you know?

Massage can help premature babies gain weight more quickly, improve their sleep patterns and release endorphins for natural pain relief. Try massaging your baby very gently before he becomes crotchety, or as a relaxant before sleep. (For more on massage see rule six: *strokes of genius*)

First aid

If you are blessed with a more-than-averagely distressed baby, what on earth can you do? We have seen some ideas for 'encompassing' (Rule Four: *You are the still waters*), but few adults have the patience to absorb all the tensions of a baby who frets for hours, day after day. American studies suggest some babies are capable for crying for an astonishing eighteen hours out of twenty-four. Becoming a new parent is hard enough for most of us, but dealing with colic or chronic illness turns the ordinary struggle into a crisis.

There are a few important ideas to help you cope, however. For instance . . .

- Do not try to go it alone. Most parents of the world consider it crazy to try to raise a baby in isolation and this rule is magnified when the baby is unsettled or able to scream at top capacity. Find a holding buddy – a best friend, babysitter, granny or neighbour – who will take over for an hour or so every day. Insist your partner does his fair share. And make the most of any free time to escape the house if you can. Fresh air and extra sleep are particularly helpful. *If you don't take care of yourself, you will not be able to take care of your baby.*

This is a preliminary condition of parenting in most cultures and we ignore it at our peril.

- Explore remedial therapies, such as gentle baby massage. To soothe a colicky baby, gently stroke his hands, one after the other, in a clockwise motion. This will help settle tensions in his tummy.

- Swaddling is an ancient art that can help to relax some persistently crying babies. (see Rule Six: *Snug as a bug*)

- Consider some of the medicines prescribed for colic. These are either sedatives to induce sleep, anti-flatulents to reduce wind, or anti-spasmodics to ease muscle spasms. All the drugs carry a risk of side effects, such as irritation of the gastro-intestinal tract, depression of the nervous system and even seizures or apnoea attacks (where the baby stops breathing). Colic drops claim to disperse pockets of gas in the intestine, but there is little evidence that gas is actually the cause.

Did you know?

Some Filipino muslims say the Prophet Mohammed cried non-stop for seven days when he was three months old. He did not stop until his mother trimmed a lock of hair from his forehead. Today, babies of the samal tribe have their locks trimmed in a commemorative ceremony – in a ritual attempt to prevent their tears.

The cutting edge

Parents everywhere will tell you with some pride that their crotchety babies are teething, but are they right? Is tooth-cutting a painful occupation which can be blamed for long months of infant crying – or is it a catch-all condition that doesn't really exist?

Back in the eighteenth century, the English doctor John Arbuthnot offered the following list of teething symptoms: 'irritation of the tender nervous parts of the jaw, occasioning inflammation, fevers, convulsions, gangrene, etc.'. Even today, people ascribe fits and fevers, diarrhoea and rashes to teething.

Teething is a near-invisible activity, which is why it is so easily blamed for crying and a thousand other symptoms. Parents claim their babies are miserable for months before and after actual teeth burst, white and serrated, from the gums. But repeated research suggests that most of the symptoms we identify with teething are nothing to do with it. Apparently those bright red circles on the cheeks, snuffles and tetchy tears cannot be put down to teething problems at all. Researchers claim the actual symptoms of teething are rather mild and – at worst – cause minor discomfort.

This, of course, does not explain the perfectly reasonable symptoms of dribbling and chewing, inflamed gums and crotchety behaviour as baby's molars cut through. Even the most strict researcher would have to concede that a baby is entitled to grouch whenever his gums are sore.

To soothe your baby's teething troubles, you could:

- Gently massage his gums with a clean finger – use a little anaesthetic teething gel if the pain seems really bad.
- Soothe dribble rash around his mouth using petroleum jelly.
- Offer a chilled teething ring or flannel – or a stick of carrot for the older baby.

> ## Did you know?
>
> A few babies are born with natal teeth already poking through, while others are still toothless at fourteen months. In the Middle Ages mothers were warned not to wean their babies until the milk teeth came through, or their babies would suffer from fevers and aching gums.

The irritated baby

Sometimes, there is an external cause for crying. If you are faced with a perpetually wretched baby, you will obviously need to check whether there is a physical trigger. Here is a list of irritants known to make babies cry. It may be that you can do something quite simple to ease his distress . . .

- Air fresheners can make babies (and parents!) quite ill, inducing symptoms such as ear infections and diarrhoea. It is best not to spray any aerosol around your baby as he is highly sensitive to the air he breathes.
- Cow's milk is the substance which upsets babies more than any other. It may be the indigestible milk proteins which are to blame – or lactose (cow's milk sugar). Take advice from your doctor before changing the formula, however, as this allergy is still quite rare. Some breastfed babies even react to the milk and cheese their mothers digest. Many mothers find their babies calm down when they cut dairy products from their diet.
- A baby with peanut allergy (or similar) may react badly to his mother's diet even before he has tasted a peanut. Nursing mothers of highly allergic babies often report

constant crying in the early months, long before weaning. If you are a big peanut fan – and especially if you ate
lots of peanuts during pregnancy – try cutting them out
of your diet for a while. If you see an improvement, talk
to your doctor about testing and the steps you will need
to take to protect your child in the future.

- Breastmilk contains many of the flavours and qualities of
  the food a mother eats. So it's not surprising that a few
  sensitive babies react to items in their mothers' diet. It
  may be worth leaving out a few of the main culprits for
  a while, e.g. red wine; coffee; milk and cheese; oranges;
  foods with lots of artificial flavourings.

Despite this list, most babies in our culture do not cry
out of pain or irritation, or for any other discernible reason.
They most likely cry because of a combination of factors to
do with their temperament and stage in development.

At around two months, the peak age for colic, a baby's
brain is making huge changes. He begins to act out of
choice, not just automatically – in other words, he is starting to make his own decisions and react spontaneously to
the world. Doctors now wonder if it's this early brain shift
which makes crying hard to control in sensitive babies.

And what can we conclude from the fact that colicky
crying is rare in some cultures? Babies who are carried
around from birth by a variety of willing hands, whose
mothers are supported by helpful, loving communities,
whose crying is met with an immediate cuddle or the breast
– these babies are less likely to develop colic in the first
place. When it comes to early nurture, perhaps it's time we
turned up the heat.

Did you know?

Around five per cent of babies suffer from childhood eczema, a red, itchy rash that often starts on the face and later appears on elbows and knees. Babies with eczema become understandably irritable, overheated and prone to crying at night. Remedies include Chinese herbal medicines, changes of diet, homoeopathy and gentle massage with sunflower oil or aloe vera cream.

Rule Five in a nutshell

- Colic is not a disease, but a description of severe crying symptoms which are very common in small babies. Once it has a hold, the condition is hard to soothe.
- Although babies in any culture may have colic symptoms, it is much less likely in places where babies are carried almost constantly from the start of life.
- Premature babies cry less at first and more as they develop – they respond well to forms of touch nurture.
- Teething, allergies and digestive problems are less likely to be the cause of colic than we imagine.
- Constant crying may be a kind of design fault in the immature human baby. He always grows out of it in the end.

rule six

Let the fun begin

'Just play. Have fun. Enjoy the game.'
MICHAEL JORDAN, AMERICAN BASKETBALL PLAYER

Learn some new tricks

One of the most important tasks of parenthood is to develop your own repertoire of skills. This does not mean becoming an instant expert or a perfect parent – it means having a go, making mistakes, learning on the job. By following your instincts, listening to your baby and trying out a few new ideas, you will soon get to know what works for both of you. And you should have more fun.

This process happens to all parents, but for some it is painful, slow and depressing. A crying baby can make you feel as if you are unable to do anything right – it seems as though the 'experts' have all the ammunition and you have an empty holster.

But even the act of getting it wrong can be useful. Childcare authors and mothers-in-law may have more experience than you, but *not with your baby*. They can make suggestions, of course, but only you can carry them out, adapt or ignore them! Only you know the intimate details of your baby's likes and dislikes. And you are the only expert your baby wants. He doesn't care what the books say – he just wants to get to know his very own, real family.

So learn some new tricks and try them out with joy. The mere fact of having a go will make you feel better and more able to cope. Only attempt strategies and therapies you feel happy about – babies don't appreciate carers who are reluctant or resentful. If your baby doesn't respond, that's absolutely fine: you're learning his likes and dislikes. If he does, then do more of it! That's the route to family happiness.

Did you know?

The 'solutions focus' training strategy uses a simple checklist to find out what works in business situations. It states that 1) if it ain't broke, don't fix it; 2) find out what works and do more of it; 3) if it's not working, do something different. Try applying these three rules as you respond to your baby today!

Joy division

Don't obsess about the crying. Don't think about the cure. Get into new, pleasurable habits with your baby, introducing fun and games that will improve both your lives – and incidentally soothe away the tears. Here are some babycare suggestions which work wonderfully to calm fretful babies. They also happen to be the kinds of thing that mothers all over the world do with their children every day, whether or not they cry.

- Take a bath with your baby. Japanese families have a ritual of *furo*, the family bath into which babies are welcomed, while Icelandic families gather to bathe in hot springs. But an ordinary bathtub or warm swimming pool will do just as well. Your baby loves to feel supported and enclosed by water – especially when your body is there to reassure him, your fingers to stroke him. Rather than dangling your baby precariously over the bathwater, try getting into the bath with him for a delicious, sensual, calming encounter.

- Sing with your baby. Lullabies are sung by mothers the world over, to 'lull' babies into a state of blissful serenity. Babies just love to listen to the soft tones of someone gently singing, feel the vibrations of the singer's body, enjoy the repetitions of simple, familiar songs. The range of songs around the world is amazing and it proves that babies are completely open-minded in their musical tastes. (See Rule Eight: *Songs that soothe.*)

- Dance with your baby. Australian author Pinky McKay recommends the 'colic waltz', dancing to the 3/4 beat the baby experienced in the womb. The Balinese mother pounds rice to the rhythm of local music and her baby on her hip is simultaneously soothed. Western parents put on their favourite CDs and bop around the house until the baby becomes hooked on certain tracks and bands. Rock music, with a strong bass line and primitive beat, is just as effective as seventeenth-century Baroque.

- Distract your baby. Blow gently on to his skin; tickle his tummy; rattle his rattle; make him laugh. Many babies are surprisingly easy to distract, moving from giggles to griping and back in a matter of seconds.

- Talk to your baby. Never forget the importance of your voice to your growing baby. He will love to listen to it, not necessarily for the sense you speak, but for the rhythms and familiarity. Occasionally we forget to speak to our babies, or feel silly doing so. We may be embarrassed to use babytalk even when alone with a real, live baby. In the end, it doesn't matter if you are reading a children's story, talking nonsense, or reciting the Periodic

Table of Elements (remember your chemistry?), your baby will be fascinated. He may even pause long enough to stop crying.

- Let your baby go skinny! Afternoons are a good time to creep into bed for a skinny sleep with your baby. Let him enjoy the sensation of his own unclothed body. Lay him on a terry nappy in case of accidents and use this time for cuddling, snoozing, nursing or playing, according to your mood. If you bare some skin, too, your baby and you will learn to enjoy the simple pleasures of touching and being touched, essential for healthy growth and development and for encouraging subtle communication.

Did you know?

Babies as young as seven months are able to understand the grammar of their mother tongue. By nine months, three per cent of babies utter their first word, while 10 per cent do not start speaking before 18 months. There is no hurry. Speech emerges in its own time.

Fixes and therapies

There are many patented therapies to soothe fretful babies, some of which are controversial, others common-sense. Here's a range of well-tried alternatives to consider . . .

Cranial Osteopathy
Some parents swear by this deceptively simple therapy, delivered in private clinics in Europe, America and Australia. The treatment is so subtle, it is tempting to imagine nothing is going on, although a few studies do suggest that it works. Cranial osteopaths believe birth leaves some babies with a constant feeling of pressure in the head, result-

ing in crying, screaming, colic and irritability. They use a finely developed sense of touch – an almost imperceptible head massage – to identify any stresses lingering in the baby's body and can also treat babies and children with special needs. May be most helpful where birth was difficult, including forceps and ventouse deliveries.

Homoeopathy

Another controversial therapy, but one which is guaranteed to do no damage to your child. Many parents swear by homoeopathy, which uses hyper-diluted substances to treat patients on the principle of 'like with like'. In other words, the remedy would normally produce the unwanted symptoms – but given in infinitesimal quantities, simply prompts the body to do its own healing. It is possible to use homoeopathy at home to treat children symptomatically, but babies and anyone with a chronic condition should always see a classically trained, registered homoeopath. Breastfed babies may be treated through the mother.

Herbal remedies

Herbs have been used for millennia to treat the whole range of human illnesses. All herbs must be used with caution as they can be as potent as any over-the-counter drug. Mothers in Germany and Austria give their colicky babies chamomile and fennel teas, which are said to soothe and lull them to sleep. But breastfed babies are best given their herbs through the mother's diet. The ancient art of Traditional Chinese Medicine (TCM) is increasingly popular in Western countries and this uses herbs to treat babies for colic, fussiness and a range of other conditions. Always seek the advice of a trained herbalist.

Did you know?

In the past, mothers used milk of magnesia to calm
their babies, but beware: it can cause diarrhoea! One
way for nursing mums to increase their babies'
magnesium levels is to eat more leafy vegetables,
which are rich in the mineral.

Strokes of genius

Massage is probably the single most important babycare
skill for new parents to master. It has been used throughout
history and in almost every culture to soothe, pacify and
delight babies.

I used to worry that massage was a complicated skill,
requiring the hands of trained professionals using exotic
oils. But you don't need fancy moves when massaging a
baby: in any case, their delicate skin must not be kneaded
or pulled around. And it's best to avoid essential oils
altogether, as the distilled aromas can be far too potent. All
babies want – in fact, crave – is the kind of light-fingered
touch you would instinctively use when stroking or soothing them.

Massage centres a baby, making his whole body shiver
and settle with joy. In some traditional cultures, babies are
treated to three or more massages a day – mothers, grandmothers, big sisters and brothers are unstinting in their
tactile affection towards the youngest member of the family.
Some people say massage makes a baby more beautiful;
others use it to heal headaches and stomach aches claiming
it helps develop the baby's central nervous system and eases
his crying.

Massage is such an important part of babycare in some

societies that people even give spiritual reasons for it. The Zinacanteco tribe of Mexico believe a baby must be massaged frequently to help him secure his soul. Mothers in Fiji massage their babies just before they go to sleep.

The human baby is much more touch-sensitive than his hairy cousin, the monkey. Massage helps to restore the balance of a baby's health and it undoubtedly works to calm crying, whether used as a preventive measure, or after the baby has become fretful.

Did you know?

Baby massage is a matter of gently caressing the baby's skin. Try sitting on the floor in a darkened room, your baby wrapped in a soft towel, cradled in the crook of your body. Ask your baby if he would like a massage – he will soon learn to communicate his readiness. Oil your hands with a little almond oil and stroke your baby with your fingertips. Only continue for as long as he seems to be enjoying it.

Snug as a bug

We've all heard of 'swaddling clothes' from Bible stories and some of us may have an image of the swaddling bands that used to be wrapped around babies as long as 4,000 years ago. But few parents are aware that swaddling remained popular in many societies until quite recently. Yet hardly any Western babies are now seriously swaddled from birth.

The art of swaddling died out only a generation or two ago, and yet for hundreds, even thousands of years, it was thought to be essential to babies' physical health. It was believed that a baby had to be wrapped tightly in many layers, like a miniature mummy, or else he would catch a chill from draughts, he would become stiff and ill-formed and – worst of all – he would cry.

Swaddling was used by parents to dampen their baby's reactions to the world. It made the baby more passive. Rather than being carried in a sling, bound to his mother's body – as he would have been in Africa and other warm climates – the swaddled baby was bound to himself, in layer upon layer of linen. In medieval Britain, for instance, it would take a nurse two hours to swaddle the baby, from his undershirt, petticoat and belly band, to the cloth nappy, head cap, straitjacket and swaddling bands. He would even have a 'stayband' attaching his cap to his shoulders, so his head could not turn in either direction.

The result was an immobile parcel which could be hung from a hook on the kitchen ceiling to stew in its own 'nourishing' juices (this was thought to be good for baby, too.) If medieval mothers were looking for peace and quiet, their method usually worked. Modern studies show that swaddling slows down baby's heartbeat, steadies his breathing and induces hours of artificially deep sleep.

Swaddling fell out of fashion in many countries, although it is still popular in Russia and a few other places. Problems with the system include an increase in body sores, and lack of tactile human contact. When you think about it, the sling-bound baby gets all the reassurance of being tightly enclosed, coupled with the movement and reassurance of his mother's body. The swaddled baby misses out on the cuddles and contact which carrying implies. And while some babies like the comfort of being tightly bound after the restriction of the womb, others resist being wrapped up.

However, there certainly is a place for swaddling in our hectic, hurried, over-stimulated world. If your baby cries a lot, it may be that he longs more than most for the sheltered security of the womb. Binding his arms to his sides and bundling him in swathes of material may be just the kind of remedial treatment he seeks. And even if swaddling itself does not calm him, it may help him to focus on the lullabies and gentle rocking motions you use to soothe away his tears.

Some doctors say swaddling works because it imitates the conditions of the womb, where the baby's arms and legs are folded against his body. They say babies do not always like the strange sensation of their own limbs flailing about in space. Some sensitive babies may be overwhelmed by the sensory messages their hands and feet send to the brain. Wrapping the baby tightly may stop him from becoming overloaded, distressed and fretful.

Swaddling has always been a controversial form of baby care: while eighteenth century childcare writers campaigned to abolish it, some modern authors are now campaigning for its return. The answer, as always, lies not with the experts, but with the highly individual preferences of your own baby. If you feel your crying infant might like the security of being wrapped up tight, try the simple method overleaf. But be aware that many babies prefer the freedom to explore the world through the spontaneous movement of their own fingers and toes. And many of them would prefer to be slung against your mobile body than to be wrapped up and left alone.

Did you know?

A simple way to swaddle: take a square baby sheet
and fold the top corner down to the centre point. Lay
baby on the sheet with his neck in line with the top
edge. Hold one arm down and fold sheet in on that
side, tucking it into his body on the other side. Bring
the bottom corner up over baby's feet and wrap the
final corner around, securing the second arm and
tucking into the finished parcel. It's ok if baby's legs
are bent but his arms should be straight.

Every little thing you do is magic

The next time you send up a little prayer for your unhappy
baby, think of all the parents around the world who do the
same. 'Spiritual babycare' may not be a chapter in your
average childcare manual, but it is completely routine in
cultures from Africa to South America, the Far East to
Australia.

I am not necessarily suggesting that you copy the
following crying cures at home. But you might like to
create your own rituals, in a supreme effort to 'magic'
away the tears. We all need a little divine intervention
from time to time . . .

- On the Japanese island of Okinawa, there's an ancient
  ritual to stop newborn babies from crying. It begins at
  ebb tide, when old women of the village circle the house
  where a new baby has been born. They clap, bang pots
  and pans and call out: 'May this baby always laugh and
  be pleasant!' The baby's grandmother wraps the placenta
  in rice straw and buries it outside near the hearth. A

stone is placed over the spot to ensure the baby will not jump in his sleep.

- In Siberia, the Mansi tribe say night-time crying is caused by the soul of an ancestor who has entered the baby's body. They hold a ritual to discover the name of the ancestor, who will leave the baby and allow him to stop crying.

- Seri women in New Mexico take twigs from the nest of 'the bird who sleeps in the afternoon' and burn them in four small piles around the crying baby. As the smoke rises, the mother sings an incantation, calling on the bird's spirit to ease her baby's tears.

Did you know?

Faith and magic play a vital part in healing and have done throughout human history. In ancient cultures, the shaman (magic man or woman) would undergo rituals on behalf of the ill or crying baby. Even today, when we kiss away our children's pains, we are enacting an ancient ritual of symbolically sucking out the poison or bad spirit that has entered through the skin. Believing in our power to heal our children is a vital part of caring for them.

Rule Six in a nutshell

- Don't be afraid to try out new ideas. Your baby will soon let you know what he enjoys and every 'mistake' is a valuable lesson in getting to know your own baby.
- Relax, let your hair down, and your baby will enjoy the fun.
- Try bathing with your baby, dancing with your baby . . . anything that enriches your lives.
- Make massage a part of your daily routine – it will calm your baby and fine-tune his system.
- Learn the ancient art of swaddling for soothing the unsettled baby.
- Explore alternative remedies if they attract you and help you create your own rituals. For thousands of years, parents have used prayers and charms to magic away the tears.

rule seven

Give generously!

Formula one

I am passionate about breastfeeding, but I also passion-
ately believe that mothers should not feel any guilt or
sense of failure for bottle-feeding their babies. We all
know that breastmilk is best and most of us try to provide
it. The fault lies not with women who endure pain, embar-
rassment and misery in the attempt to nurse, but with our
society which still does not know how to provide the right
support.

Whatever your choices, whatever your circumstances,
your baby needs you to put any regrets or doubts behind
you. And you certainly don't need some childcare author
telling you you've got it all wrong. In the end, bottle-
feeding and breastfeeding are details – it's how we deliver
them that matters.

So if you are formula-feeding your baby, don't bottle it
up. There is no reason why your baby should miss out on
any of the cuddles, caresses and kindnesses that seem to
come automatically with breastfeeding. The more tender-
ness you show your baby, the more subtle your communication and the less crying there should be.

Here are some suggestions for formula-feeding with
panache . . .

- Always cuddle your baby while feeding and look into his eyes. Try not to leave him alone with his bottle or turn him to face away from you.
- Let your baby caress your skin while he feeds. Shed a layer of clothing to make the feeds more intimate.
- Anticipate feeds before your baby starts to cry, so he does not learn to howl before teatime. Swift soothing reduces crying.
- Long feeding intervals lead to a more frenzied, windy feeding style. It becomes especially important to let your baby feed in an upright position and give him the chance to burp afterwards if he needs it.

Occasionally it's the formula that causes the crying. Most powdered formulas are based on cow's milk, a substance designed for the rapid growth of baby cows, not the healthy development of human babies. Goat's milk is nearer the mark and gorilla milk would be the best of all animal substitutes! But you can't domesticate a gorilla or induce it to produce a commercial yield. The reason your baby is on cow's milk is because it's easy to farm cows.

Having only one stomach (unlike calves, which have two), some babies find bovine milk – with its indigestible fatty acids, iron and protein – understandably difficult to down. It takes four hours for the baby's body to digest formula milk, compared with twenty minutes for breast-milk. Studies suggest that bottle-fed babies are, for instance, more than three times as likely to be admitted to hospital with severe respiratory tract illnesses than breastfed babies. It may be the milk that's doing it.

Yet many doctors are sceptical about suggesting a change of formula, even for a windy or colicky baby. They point out that infant crying often settles down by the age of three months, around the time when formulas are changed. They are not convinced about cause and effect. And some babies are even more reactive to alternative soya milks than they are to the original brand.

You may have to trust your own instincts when it comes to an unsettled, bottle-fed baby. A change of formula may ease the crying – but perhaps the best remedy of all is to offer your baby the physical comfort which he craves just as much as food.

Did you know?

The race to create a suitable infant formula began in the 1860s, but not until the 1920s – and the advent of pasteurization – were artificial milks considered safe. Today, after continued and intensive marketing, most of the world's babies receive some chemically modified cow's milk.

Nursing from the heart

Contrary to popular opinion, pretty much every mother can breastfeed. If she can conceive, carry and give birth to her baby, nature will make sure she can suckle him, too. Unless she's had breast surgery or there is physical damage to the breast tissue and nipples, a woman is perfectly equipped to be her baby's source of sustenance for the first six months at least.

This is not what modern mothers are told and it's often not what they believe. Unfortunately, the 'belief' side of things is extremely important. The first principle of breast-feeding is to get the mind and heart fully engaged.

Whether or not you find breastfeeding easy is not down to the shape of your nipples, the difficulty of the birth, or 'how much' milk you can make (the milk supply is stimulated from day to day by the baby suckling). It has more to do with the people around you. In societies which really support breastfeeding – the ones where they give it emotional, practical and spiritual backing; where fathers and mothers-in-law are all for it and nobody nags you to stop or asks you to go away and do it in private – every woman is able to breastfeed.

Women in 100 per cent breastfeeding cultures (and there are lots) don't worry about minor problems like engorgement or where tomorrow's milk will come from. If they encounter problems, they and everyone around them just assume they will keep going. It's the support which makes the difference.

Researchers in many traditional cultures have observed that mothers nurse their babies little and often, as soon as the baby niggles or cries. They don't limit the number of feeds they give by watching clocks or following schedules. This approach sounds time-consuming, but it does work. Demand nursing – including a quick response – is the way that breastfeeding evolved through human history. It is the way nursing works best today. The benefits of demand feeding include:

- Babies stimulate just the amount of milk they need for the next day.
- They put on weight more rapidly.
- Crying is reduced.
- Mothers experience fewer problems with swollen breasts and blocked milk ducts.
- Periods are delayed and there is an increased contraceptive effect.

One study of breastfeeding American mothers compared those who nursed at long intervals (three or more hours between each feed) and those who fed their babies on demand. The quietest babies were those who were fed at short intervals *and* whose mothers responded quickly to any crying. This was the most effective combination of all. Mothers who responded swiftly but nursed at long intervals and mothers who responded slowly but nursed at short intervals all had to deal with more crying from their babies.

Giving generously is written into the small print of successful breastfeeding. All those rules about limiting the number and length of feeds – especially a ban on night-time nursing – help to disturb and even sabotage the process. Babies like to be fed little and often and *right now*!

There are other considerations, like allowing the baby to open his mouth wide and suckle from the areola, the dark area around the nipple, not merely from the nipple itself. But once you have the knack of nursing, the single most important issue is generosity of spirit. Nursing your baby is an act of love.

Did you know?

Newborn babies who are allowed to nurse at will and sleep next to their mothers do not always lose weight after birth. Research on babies born at home in london showed – given lots of skin-to-skin contact and free access to the breast day and night – that some babies managed to avoid the usual neonatal weight loss. They maintained their birthweight for three days before starting to gain.

Tears before teatime

We have already seen how crying is just one side of an ancient call-and-response system. Human babies are born so immature that they need an alarm to bring their parents running at the slightest hitch. Simply being alone can be enough to trigger tears for the average baby. But the single most common reason for crying is the baby's need to suckle.

Current breastfeeding advice tends to divide suckling into two different categories: hunger versus comfort. We are supposed to limit baby's time at the breast in case he spends too long merely sucking when he is no longer hungry. Yet the desire for comfort-sucking (and for the caresses which go with it) is absolutely enormous for the tiny baby. In tests, crying babies are more easily soothed by being held in human arms – even if they have to wait for food – than they are by being artificially fed until their stomachs are full, without the benefit of being held.

Mothers in many other cultures do not ask themselves why a baby wants to suckle so often. They cannot measure the amount of milk a baby needs, so tend to presume that all nursing is a good thing. Perhaps they do know that the newborn baby has a stomach the size of a walnut. He needs to be fed frequently and cannot take in much milk at a time.

Babies who cry a lot are inevitably viewed as 'difficult', but one interesting study suggests that crying can actually be good for babies, helping them survive in critical situations. In the 1970s, Dutch researcher Marten de Vries observed Masai babies in Kenya, labelling them 'difficult' (i.e. babies that cried more) or 'easy' (i.e. passive and quiet.) When he returned three months later, he found that seven out of the thirteen study babies had died during a terrible drought. Amazingly, only one of these was a baby he had previously labelled 'difficult'. The other six fatalities had all been in the 'easy' category.

Crying invites nurture. It forces parents to take notice of the baby, to attempt to pacify him with extra feeds, stimulation and care. In some circumstances, crying really can be good for your baby. When yours is crying his heart out, think to yourself: perhaps my baby is the most intelligent on the block. He's a survivor.

Did you know?

A study of mothers and newborn babies in Jamaica showed that those babies who cried before breastfeeding put on more weight than those babies who did not cry first. This may mean a number of things: crying prompts mothers to nurse / hungry babies cry more / the loudest babies are more likely to get their needs met.

The rainforest effect

Crying and breastfeeding go together in a very specific way. Scientists tell us that the sound of her baby's voice, including the crying, helps to stimulate a mother's 'milk ejection reflex'. In fact, a newly delivered mother can use her baby's first cries to help to initiate nursing. It's an instinctive and hormonal reaction which produces a tingling in the nipples and areola and can even make the breasts ache.

So crying is a baby's way of switching his mother 'on' for breastfeeding. It is not, however, the only way of encouraging the milk flow. Studies from America show that skin-to-skin contact also excites the release of milk in a lactating woman. In some cultures, midwives give new mothers regular breast massages to encourage milk production.

Bathing is also a stimulant, especially when the breasts are sponged during the bath or shower – but soap should not be used as its artificial scent is off-putting to the baby. The sound of running water is another trigger, and so is warmth: mothers in the mountainous region of Guatemala believe the cold climate can turn their milk 'sour'. They heat their homes with rocks before they begin nursing.

Before *you* begin nursing, you might imagine yourself in the rainforest, gathering your crying baby in your arms, skin-to-skin in the warm, humid atmosphere. Trees are rustling outside (leave the heating on and windows open) and there's the sound of a running spring (experiment with the bath taps!). You do not even need to put your breast in your baby's mouth – it is not a bottle, after all – just relax and wait until he turns his head and opens his mouth as wide as a fledgling bird. Let him take the breast for himself. This is the call-and-response system in full motion.

Did you know?

Babies who fuss after feeding may prefer a more upright nursing position. If your baby lies on his back he takes in more wind (imagine if you were expected to digest your meals lying down or with your head back!). A bloated stomach leads to the gas which gives a baby digestive pain. Better to let your baby's body dangle down as much as possible, just as babies do when they nurse on the move in nomadic societies – and as they evolved to do throughout human history. When they feed in this position babies rarely need burping at all.

Peace and quiet

The world's favourite way of stopping a baby crying is to stick something in his mouth. If it isn't the breast, it's a breast substitute – a dummy or pacifier, usually made out of rubber with a small plastic loop on the end.

Western culture has mixed feelings about the dummy – plenty of children use them, but their parents have to weather the disapproval of other parents and doctors. Yet studies show that giving a baby a pacifier does work, just as well, in fact, as picking up the baby or nursing. The baby's need to suckle is intense and begins in the womb, when he begins to suck his thumb or the back of his hand and comfort himself.

So the pacifier literally brings peace and quiet. Parents in previous generations knew this too: in eighteenth-century Russia, for instance, babies were given a cloth bag filled with a bread-and-milk mixture to suck on. On the other hand, mothers in many cultures manage completely without dummies, because they allow their babies frequent access to the breast.

And medical arguments don't favour the pacifier. Apart from the question of hygiene (dummies occasionally land on the floor before being returned to the desperate baby's mouth), there is plenty of evidence that they interfere with development.

Dummies affect speech and language learning in small children. Instead of listening to his own babbling, the baby is rendered artificially quiet. His parents or caretakers are less likely to chat to him, as he is unable to respond. Rubber teats – like thumb-sucking – can change the shape of the baby's palate, which can alter his speech patterns and the way his teeth grow. Dummies also stop babies putting objects into their mouths when they get to that stage of development: they disturb the baby's evolved way of exploring his world.

Finally, breastfeeding is at risk when babies use a dummy for more than two hours a day – on a very simple level, the baby needs to suck on the breast to generate the hormones that make the next day's milk. If he is sucking on something else, the signals won't get through.

It is tempting to give your baby a dummy when he is crying and you need some peace. Using a dummy is hardly a crime. But the pacifier will always be a substitute for a more yielding, tactile, sensory from of comfort: the human breast.

Did you know?

Only two per cent of Japanese babies are given a dummy, compared with more than 80 per cent of Austrian babies. Although many Austrian mothers breastfeed, they tend to believe that a baby cannot manage without a pacifier. Doctors are campaigning to convince them otherwise.

Don't spoil the fun!

One of the most popular arguments for not answering a crying baby is that by meeting all his demands we will spoil him. Parents who might otherwise have been happy to carry their babies around, nurse them frequently and fall hopelessly in love are encouraged to hold back on their generosity, in case their child keeps on demanding when he grows up. Phrases like 'He'll wrap you round his little finger' encourage mothers to feel enslaved to babies when meeting their most basic needs.

This attitude completely misses the point about babies.

Newborn and small infants are not ten-year-old children or lazy adults: they are a species apart, with a set of needs specific to their own age group. When a baby cries – in other words, asks for something – he is not trying to manipulate or trick you. His demands, his needs, his wants are not whimsical, they are vital to his well-being and long-term health.

When you meet a baby's fundamental demands, you make him feel whole. He will not gloat at his victory or understand your sense of sacrifice, he will just feel right. Giving to a baby is like filling a car full of petrol. He depends on your generosity for his survival. And he must keep refuelling again and again until he can manage by himself. In this way, you are also guaranteeing his fitness for the future.

When we thwart or ignore a baby's cries, we teach him a very strange lesson indeed: that trying to communicate is hopeless. He will not realize that he has washed up in a country and century where it is the fashion to 'teach' him to be prematurely independent. Repeatedly ignoring a baby's cries makes him feel at odds, unfulfilled, desperate even. He has begun an unnecessary battle with the world. He learns to cry quickly for even the most ordinary things. Or he learns not to cry at all.

One of the saddest situations for a human baby is to be left almost entirely without human contact. Babies in orphanages and old-fashioned institutions are prone to a condition known as 'infant marasmus', a wasting disease where they become listless and apathetic. They stop crying, they stop reacting to the world. They look, to all intents and purposes, depressed.

Ordinary babies in ordinary homes receive too much stimulation and attention to be at risk of depression. But we should never be sceptical about their cries for attention, for cuddling, for nursing, for joining in with human activity. These are the things a baby was born for. One day, your child will grow out of all this demanding, and you will be able to encourage him to rely on his own resources. Meanwhile, go on: spoil him all you like.

Did you know?

Japanese parents (like other parents around the world) do not aim to make their children independent, but inter-dependent. This means emphasizing community values, such as giving, sharing, caring and co-operating. Babies are allowed their amae – dependency – and everyone is delighted to help meet their early needs.

Rule Seven in a nutshell

* If you are going to bottle-feed, do it with confidence and panache, not guilt or regret. Bottle-fed babies enjoy the same tactile contact as breastfed babies.
* We know breastfeeding is good for babies, but mothers need more support in order to be able to give freely and make it work.
* Frequent nursing coupled with a quick response reduces crying.
* In a crisis, crying can be good for babies, as it encourages mothers to feed them and meet their needs. The baby puts out lots of sensual triggers to make the mother produce milk.
* You cannot spoil a baby by giving him limitless love and attention.

rule eight

Give in to good sleep

'Maybe your child's brain was designed by natural selection over millions of years during which mothers slept with their babies. Maybe back then if babies found themselves completely alone at night it often meant something horrific had happened – the mother had been eaten by a beast, say. Maybe the young brain is designed to respond to this situation by screaming frantically so that any relatives within earshot will discover the child. Maybe, in short, the reason that kids left alone sound terrified is that kids left alone naturally get terrified. Just a theory.'

ROBERT WRIGHT, AMERICAN AUTHOR

The human cradle

Crying is a baby's most alert state: his body becomes completely agitated. Sleep is his most passive state – for parents, it means minimum trouble. No wonder parents spend so long trying to persuade their babies to stop crying and start sleeping. And then, perhaps, they can get a little sleep themselves . . .

We may not realize it, but half our parenting is done at night. Whether your baby sleeps in a distant nursery or close by in your bedroom, can make a huge difference to his early life experiences – and yours! Traditionally, babies always slept with their mothers and other family members at close quarters, so mothers could breastfeed without having to wake up properly or even get out of bed.

The ancient human art of 'co-sleeping' is the way that babies evolved. It is also a strikingly simple way to reduce crying. Many babies who sleep next to their parents never need to cry at all. Their parents, meanwhile, need hardly wake up and they certainly don't have to stir out of bed.

The way it works is this: small babies depend on human contact for their sense of well-being. When sleeping near their parents (or others) they benefit from all sorts of subtle stimulation: the movement of another body, the warm, tactile contact of skin, the sounds people make and the air they breathe out. Most importantly, the nursed baby also has ready access to the breast.

Scientists studying cot death now realize that all these things contribute to the baby's overall health, reminding him to keep breathing, sleep more steadily, regulate his body temperature and finally wake without trauma or a rise in his stress hormones. Babies do not need hours and hours of deep sleep – in fact, it can be quite dangerous for them – but a light, touch-sensitive environment that helps to remind them to stay alive.

The current consensus is that humans were designed for light sleep. Each of us wakes up around thirty-seven times in the night (every thirteen minutes!), mostly without realizing it. Light sleep helps to protect us, keeping us aware of any dangers in the environment. We need to be able to respond to tigers, or fires, or more modern catastrophes. And for babies, light sleep is even more critical – it helps them to reconnect with their parents, to feed, to keep breathing.

Contrary to popular wisdom, the problem is not the waking we do, but our inability to get off to sleep again. In some tribes, people wake in the night to share a joke and then doze off as suddenly as they awoke. In our society, where children are often left to cry when they wake, they rarely get to practise their inborn skill of dropping off quickly. They are taught to sleep in laboratory-like conditions: lights out, firm mattress and pillows just so. Despite the fact that all the rest of the world sleeps together, we insist that our babies and children sleep alone.

Nature designed babies with an expectation of someone to sleep with. So they often protest when they are put down to sleep alone, or wake to find no one there. Sleep problems and crying go hand in hand. Reams have been written on how to train babies to sleep alone – and then how to handle the screaming, the head-banging, the self-comforting, the nightmares and the insecurities which are apt to follow.

It surprises many western parents to learn that in almost every other culture in the world, from Africa to Asia and South America, such sleep problems do not exist. Babies sleep near their parents and drift in and out of sleep, suffering no more trauma than they did when they slept in the womb. And, once they adjust to the tiny sounds and fluttering movements of a baby nearby, their parents are able to sleep too . . .

Did you know?

A study of ninety different cultures around the world revealed that in seventy-one, parents still routinely slept with their babies. In another study of middle-class British families, only 18 per cent of mothers who slept with their babies actually admitted as much to their doctors.

Pillow talk

Safety of the vulnerable baby is paramount, and every parent wants to know how best to protect the precious newborn. When they consider the idea of sleeping near their baby, most parents' first concern is that they might roll over and harm him. But many hours of research prove that parents don't generally roll over on their babies in the night. If they did, the human race wouldn't have survived today. Video tapes show how mothers care for their babies even while they sleep: cooling them down, stroking them, nursing and moving them around.

Even so, there are some fairly obvious safety rules to observe when taking a baby into your bed. Most importantly, do not sleep with your baby if you or your partner are:

SMOKING
DRUNK OR DRUGGED
TOO ILL TO TAKE RESPONSIBILITY FOR YOUR BABY
SLEEPING ON A SOFA OR POLYSTYRENE-FILLED CUSH-
IONS

Or if your baby is:
VERY ILL (although co-sleeping may be just what your baby needs. If in doubt ask your GP.)
IN A SPLINT
SWADDLED – i.e. unable to move

Here are some other night-time tips:

- Babies do not need pillows. Keep these away from your baby's head.
- Do not wrap the baby up too warmly – remember the benefits of skin-to-skin contact.
- You will need a very dim light in your room: just enough to check your baby and tend to him.
- Babies do not tend to wet the bed as they don't wake fully in the night, but you could lay an extra terry nappy underneath your baby if you like.

- Create the bedtime routines that suit you best. Much-carried babies do not generally depend on routine or need a comfort object.
- Be firm about bedtime etiquette – do not let your baby take over the centre of the bed while you cling to the sides. As he gets older, make it clear that he is welcome so long as he doesn't wake you up.

Lots of parents worry about the day when they want their bed back to themselves, fearing that the child will never move out into his own space. We must remember that to give a child security makes him more secure; to feed his early dependency makes him – in the end – more independent. Weaning the baby out of the bed is a process, much like weaning on to solids, out of nappies, or into school.

The art of stress-free parenting is to go with the flow. Indulge your baby while he is small and deal with each stage of development as it arises, not before. We should not always live as if the worst will happen. These may be the best years of their lives.

Did you know?

One of the biggest reasons for a drop in sexual libido after birth is lack of sleep. If sleeping near your baby means you are not woken in the night, you should find you have more energy for your partner. Try to find time in the evening to spend together and rekindle the romance. Your baby's early evening sleep is a good time for this. You may want to put him down in another room so you can have privacy and time alone.

The original night nurse

Night nursing, healthy sleeping and reduced crying: these three little items go together like gems in a perfect setting. Babies need to feed around the clock and *that* is one of the main reasons why they wake at night and alert us to their state of panic and abandonment.

Meanwhile, mothers are programmed to doze while tending to their nursing babies. Hormonal changes mean that a nursing mother doesn't go into the fourth, or deepest, stage of sleep at all. At the same time, the action of the baby's gums against the areola (the soft brown circle around the nipple) stimulates a hormonal 'snooze button', making the mother drowsy.

These strange chemical reactions mean that nursing mothers were designed to fall asleep on the job, not tiptoe up to a beautifully decorated nursery to lower the lightly sleeping baby into a lonely crib. They mean nursing mothers were adapted to sleep lightly around their babies in order to protect them. The whole picture tells us that breast-feeding was meant to go on during the night, not just at pre-set intervals during the day.

There are a couple of major advantages to night nursing. For a start, the night feeds are the calmest ones: unwatched, unhurried, baby and mother can get into a rhythm which concerns no one but themselves. Once you learn how to lie down to feed (the post-caesarean nursing position – on your side with your upper leg supported – is ideal) baby can drink deeply from each breast. As he suckles, he becomes drowsy until he drops off. There are chemicals in breastmilk which are similar to those found in commonly prescribed tranquillizers and he enjoys their effect.

On a scientific note, night feeds produce more prolactin than day-time feeds. Prolactin is the hormone that stimulates the milk supply for the next few days. It is also the hormone that gives the mother contraceptive protection, delaying the return of her periods. This in turn helps to give her reproductive system a rest and protect against a number of different cancers.

When mothers are told they do not have 'enough' milk for their babies, does anyone check whether the baby is feeding right through the twenty-four hours? When periods return quickly and second babies are conceived sooner than planned, does anyone ask about the night feeds?

In eighteenth-century Europe, when it become the fashion to send babies out to wet-nurse, many women gave birth to twenty or more babies, one after the other without cease. Mothers who were freed from the 'burden' of breastfeeding were saddled with repeated pregnancies and perilous births.

In hunter-gatherer groups, where frequent breastfeeding is practised day and night, there is a natural break of four years between each baby. Humans were not designed to give birth to more than around seven babies in a lifetime. Even without the benefit of the pill, our species was protected against over-population and women were sheltered from excessive child-bearing.

Night nursing is part of the small print in the breastfeeding contract. By keeping your baby near you, at least you can sleep while you nurse.

Did you know?

There is no need for nursing mothers to wear a bra at night. With your baby beside you, you only have to open half an eye to feed. Then you don't have to fiddle with hooks and eyes, flaps and zips in the dark . . .

Quietness for babies

Good sleep has become a precious commodity. We suffer from lack of it ourselves and we try to induce it in our babies from the youngest age. Even newborns are put on to sleep training programmes in an effort to make them trouble-free and avoid 'problems' arising later on. Never mind that the training programmes themselves may create extra crying and problems of their own.

One way to stamp out all the crying and produce sleepy, passive babies is to drug them. There is a long and distressing history of baby-drugging which stretches all the way from the opium fields of Afghanistan – where babies in refugee camps are dosed by their desperate mothers to keep them quiet – to the sedatives and gripe waters we find in the modern medicine cabinet.

Most sedatives are based on opium. Ancient Egyptian babies were fed a mixture of poppy seeds and fly dung, a concoction which 'acts at once!' according to the Ebers Papyrus, a medical manual from around 1500 BC. From the eighteenth century onwards, half the population (including most of the babies) took opiates for whatever ailed them. In the nineteenth century, British babies were given Godfrey's Cordial, a combination of opium, treacle and water which was also known as 'Quietness' for babies. It is estimated that thousands of babies were killed every year by mothers and nurses accidentally overdosing them on over-the-counter medicines. Even today, many European babies are given opiates in their mildest form: poppyseed tea.

By the time they are eighteen months old, one quarter of all babies in Western culture have taken sedative drugs. Colic drops and paracetamol syrups, anti-histamines and teething gels all contain sedatives. We give these medicines for a variety of reasons – not only do they stop the crying, they also happen to induce sleep. It's a side effect no one is complaining about.

Used sparingly to ease pain, infant medicines can diminish symptoms and give everyone the chance to relax and take a breath. But some babies are given sedatives daily for months at a time, which can be extremely harmful. Too much paracetamol, for instance, starts to deactivate the body's own pain killers.

Before we rush to the chemist, we might remind ourselves of what we are giving our babies when we sedate them. We might, instead of trying to suppress the symptoms of a needy or sensitive baby, try a more holistic approach. Just by offering our babies the warmth of our arms and contact with our skin, we can encourage their own pain-soothing reactions, enhance their self-healing and ease their tears.

Did you know?

Nineteenth-century american parents could legitimately knock their babies out with 'cocaine toothache drops', which sold under the banner of two cute children crossing a stream. The slogan was 'instantaneous cure!' Even Coca-Cola contained cocaine until 1903.

Songs that soothe

We've talked about hushing and shushing babies, and we should not forget the ancient art of 'lulling' them to sleep. The lullaby is a universal feature of human life. All cultures have lullabies and – as far as we can make out – they always have. There is something fundamental about the simple songs that people sing to their babies to distract the tears and induce sleep.

Even in cultures where music is banned – eg. in Afghanistan during periods of religious intolerance – mothers still hum and lull sweet tunes into their babies' ears. Musicologists tell us that this intimate, early singing is the most important music lesson humans ever learn. We know that babies drink in lots of information from the first tunes they hear. Lullabies are like a first taste of their own culture.

All babies are born with perfect pitch, but most lose this skill because the voices around them are unlikely to be completely in tune. Babies are so adaptable, they retune their ears to the lullabies they are given. And this also proves that lullabies are a valuable part of the language-learning process. Babies use them to tune into the melody and accent of the mother-tongue they will soon be speaking.

Lullabies come before baby talk, before the intrusion of meaning turns our words in judgements or commands. Before parents can convey their fears and their expectations, their anger or their discipline, they use songs to convey their love.

And, of course, lullabies play an essential role in soothing the fretful baby. He responds instinctively to the soft tones, the consonants and the peaceful intentions of the end-of-day melodies that are so familiar to him. It doesn't matter how simple the lullaby may be – the only essential part is the lull-lulling. In Tibet, mothers may sing a mantra – a protective incantation with many layers of meaning – such as 'OM TARE TUTTARE TURE SOHA', over and over again. Lullabies induce a trance-like calm over the fractious child.

In most cultures, the lullaby carries little meaning beyond the ramblings of the singer's mind. Some lullabies threaten the baby with dire consequences (the cradle will fall . . .), others sing of Daddy who is far away. Some sing of their hopes for the fledging life, others are like a weather report or a description of the local landscape.

It doesn't matter what you sing about. And if you've forgotten the old songs, new ones are easily created. By repeating your favourites over and over again, you will have a ready means of soothing your baby. Nothing will ever be as special to him as your unique voice singing softly in the way only you know how. It's your very own key to unlock the crying.

Did you know?

Babies tune into all sorts of music. It's easy to get them hooked on your favourite CD, whether it's Moby or Mozart. There is even a CD called *Punk Rock Baby* which reworks the songs of The Clash and Sex Pistols in lullaby style. Repetition of old favourites can prove an instant soother for babies who find it difficult to drop off to sleep.

Rule Eight in a nutshell

- Babies evolved to sleep next to their parents or other carers at night. Most cultures sleep near or with their babies and protect their babies through the night, following common-sense rules to ensure maximum safety.
- Light, tactile sleep is good for babies, reminding them to breathe and sleep more evenly.
- Co-sleeping makes it easier to breastfeed and provides benefits for mother and baby. It also reduces crying.
- We should beware of giving our babies any medicines routinely to aid sleep or stop crying.
- Lullabies are a wonderful way of soothing crying babies and inducing peaceful sleep.

rule nine

Wear your baby well

'. . . as we were going out the door Akak grabbed her baby,
Anautalik, who was barely old enough to sit up on her
own, and slid the baby down the back of her anorak. I
watched in amazement. I had climbed in the winter season
in the Himalaya, but this blustery, moist cold here was more
penetrating and severe. It stung. I didn't know the infant
was going fishing too and was surprised, but I thought
about it and realized that Inuit infants had participated in
all events with their mothers in years past out of necessity.
So of course they could do so today just as well.'

JAN REYNOLDS, 'THE CARRYING OF INFANTS
FOR ALL TASKS WITH THE INUIT OF THE ARCTIC',
MOTHER AND CHILD, 1997

Cache and carry

So what is all the fuss about carrying babies around? Does
it really make any difference whether a baby is popped
into a pushchair or bound to your back? Isn't the back-
strapping thing a little inelegant for the modern mother-on-
the-move?

The thing is that – however we decide to bring up our
babies – their bodies were designed for a Stone Age lifestyle.
We may think modern life is hectic, but to a baby it can be
strangely static and boring. His inbuilt expectation is that
he will be born to nomadic parents who forage and hunt all
day for food, taking him along for the ride. He does not
expect to be put down for hours at a time, either for sleep
or to engage in exaggerated baby talk. And it's something

in the gap between the Stone Age and current childcare fashion that increases the chances of crying.

It would be fine to put our babies into cots and prams and baby seats all day if we were a nesting species, like the birds. But we are not. We belong to the group of primates, all of whom carry their babies around until they are mature enough to fend for themselves. And since human newborns are the least mature of the bunch, that's a lot of carrying. Traditional societies typically carry babies non-stop for the first six months or more until they can crawl or walk away. Older babies and toddlers are also carried around until they struggle to be independently mobile.

The benefits to babies are easy to chart. Human babies discharge their energy through being carried around. Begun at birth, baby-wearing may well reduce the chances of colic or pent-up evening crying.

Exercise and fresh air are vital components of a healthy life, however small the human. A lot of infant crying may result from the amount of time they spend indoors. To wear your baby out, try walking outside with him as much as you can. You may not live in the wilds or wish to scour the bushes for berries, but a trip to the corner shop will do just as well. With baby in a sling, you can both take the exercise that will help keep you fit and healthy.

Being carried enhances the baby's nervous system, controlling his sense of balance. It improves his motor development and makes him more calm. He becomes less prone to colic and wind. And he is able to see the world from a mobile vantage point – so improving his sense of spatial awareness.

Anthropologists who have compared African babies with American babies are amazed by how much more advanced the much-carried African infants seem to be. Within ten days of being constantly held and carried after birth,

African babies have better muscle tone, they are more alert and they have better social interaction scores. They are also months ahead when it comes to standing, crawling and walking.

Human babies desperately want to be carried around – in fact, as much as we are prepared to carry them. Baby monkeys book their own ride by clinging to their mothers' fur. Human babies have no such advantage. They are born with a grasping reflex, but this fades after a few days or weeks. It's hard to grip on to a furless mother, in any case.

After the grasping reflex has disappeared, a baby has two ways of appealing to be carried: his endearing smile and his piercing cry. He is prepared to use either or both in his effort to communicate his needs.

There may be reasons – a bad back, disability – why you are unable to carry your baby on a sling or in your arms. Don't despair! Your baby will appreciate any loving touch you are able to offer and he will also love to be held by others. Enrol Grandpa or big sister, your best friend or partner to do as much holding as they can. Your baby will be one of the most sociable and adored creatures for miles.

Did you know?

For many traditional peoples, baby-carrying is an honour and people beg to be allowed to have their turn. Big sister or brother is often given the role of child nurse. In Nigeria, Kenya and other African countries, a bond is forged through carrying that is never forgotten. Adults often introduce older siblings as 'the brother (or sister) who carried me'.

Slings you should know

- An Ethiopian baby rides high on his mother's back, in a pouch encircled by a muslin cape that goes over her shoulders. If it rains, the mother carries her umbrella over both of them. As a child gets older, he learns to sit between his mother's shoulder blades, clinging with his legs around her waist.
- Fulani babies of Nigeria are carried in large, bright cotton wraps, which are bound around the mother's torso and enable the infant to enjoy a secure piggy-back.
- Swazi babies of Swaziland are carried on their mothers' backs in a goatskin sling. This is traditionally a gift from the new mother's parents.
- In Liberia, west Africa, the Kpelle people grow cotton and weave it into distinctive stripes. Women wear a two-yard strip called a *lapa,* wrapped around the body under the arms, with a smaller piece of cloth which ties at the waist and holds baby on the back.
- In medieval France, babies were slung in a bundle or *trousse* on their mothers' bodies and taken everywhere.
- In Wales, a mother would carry her baby wrapped against her in a shawl. The English-speaking Welsh still use a dialect phrase, 'cutching up', which refers to the closeness of the carried baby.
- Babies in Morocco are carried in slings on the back.
- Maori mothers in New Zealand would traditionally carry their babies in swag straps made from pounded bark.
- Sub-arctic tribes, stretching from Alaska to Labrador, have carried their babies in elaborately beaded belts since the nineteenth-century. Beadwork was taught to the Cree, the Slave, the Dogrib and others by settlers from Europe.

- In southern India, the baby is worn next to the skin, under the top section of the mother's sari. In other places, he may be transported in a wrap on the front or side.
- Andaman islanders of the Bay of Bengal have an ancient tradition involving a baby sling. When a pregnancy is deeply desired, especially by the husband, he sits around the camp wearing an empty baby sling. This symbol of maternity, usually worn by mothers, will help bring a rapid conception.
- A baby from Bali is wrapped against his mother using a cloth shawl.
- Nomad mothers of Tibet place babies skin-to-skin under their sheepskin coats.
- Hmong parents of Laos in south-east Asia carry their babies in beautifully embroidered cloth slings called *nyias*. An expectant mother will sew the *nyia* during pregnancy, embellishing it with sacred motifs to help protect her baby's soul.
- In China, babies are traditionally bound to their mother's backs with hemp cloth bands. The baby's back is supported with a stiffened pad and hemp is wound round the two of them: crossing over at the front of the mother's body and finally tied at the waist. Another piece of hemp may be used as a baby hat for warmth, or as a sun-shade.
- Slings are back in vogue. Recent fashions include a leather and sheepskin papoose, as modelled by the babies of David and Victoria Beckham. (Don't mention it, but these are exactly the materials used by ancient hunter-gatherers when they first made slings for carrying their Stone Age babies around.)

Did you know?

To avoid a bad back, find a sling that wraps around your body without buckles or metal fixings. It is important the baby doesn't drag down at the front, causing your shoulders to sag and the small of your back to ache. Slings that wrap round your body and your baby's torso help to support you both as you move.

Heart to heart

It's a female thing. Mothers tend to carry their babies on the left. But why do we do this and how might it help to soothe our fretful babies?

Scientists have calculated that 83 per cent of right-handed mothers – and 78 per cent of left-handed – habitually hold their babies on the left-hand side. Even girls playing with their dolls tend to cradle them using the left arm, which suggests that this instinct is very deep-rooted. Men and boys, by contrast, show no particular preference for left-handed holding.

Researchers believe this behaviour is not merely designed to leave the right hand free for doing other things (although this might also be part of nature's design.) They point out that, since babies are calmed by listening to the mother's heart beat in the womb, they can more easily be soothed this way after birth.

They also notice that, with his right ear jammed against his mother's body, the baby's left ear is automatically free. The left ear is connected to the right side of the brain, which processes emotions and helps the baby interpret his parents' affection. Meanwhile, mother looks down at her baby using the left-hand side of her face, so she connects with equal emotion to him.

It's not just that mothers insist on holding their babies on the left – babies prefer it. They tend to present their left side to mum! There are lots of reasons for this. For the majority, a right-hand preference is developed by the twenty-ninth week of pregnancy. Sixty per cent of unborn babies lie with their right sides close to the outer wall of the womb, where they will receive more stimulation.

Then, a baby is born with slightly more nerves leading to the brain from the right-hand side of his body. And he is equipped with a 'tonic neck reflex' – i.e. a preference for turning his head to the right. This gives a slight twist to his body which makes him more likely to become right-handed. And if he is carried on the left a lot, he will also – in due course – become more 'left eared', i.e. use his left ear for listening to the world. Scientists say this helps us to process the emotion behind each conversation.

For the human baby, all these lefts and rights should – paradoxically – lead to a more balanced existence. Chimpanzees and gorillas always carry their babies on the left and so do most ancient hunter-gatherer tribes, like the San people of the Kalahari Desert in Africa. (San babies nurse from the left breast while on the move and from the right when the mother is stationary.) The left-brain/right-hand solution ought to lead to a life approach that is at once emotional and practical.

It ought also to help parents soothe their babies when they are distressed. By passing our babies on the left-hand side, we can relate to their emotions with more empathy and they, in turn, will learn to read our love and concern for them. This is one of those wonderful examples where information and intuition meet to make perfect sense.

Did you know?

The Talmud, the ancient book of Jewish law, says 'a woman who begins to nurse her son should start on the left side, as the source of all understanding is from the left.'

Life does go on!

One of the main concerns of the modern mother is how she can make life a little easier for herself. This is not because she is lazier than all the generations of women who have gone before, but because she is called upon to play too many roles, unsupported by public opinion, community care or a daily maid. We may have more gadgets and a better standard of living than our grandmothers, but we also lead more splintered lives. And when it comes to parenting, we are expected to cope, cope well and cope alone.

The idea of carrying a baby around for most of the day therefore comes as a bit of a shock to the new parent who was planning to keep her baby's demands under control. But equally shocking is the amount of crying a baby can do when he is left, sleepless, in a cot for hours at a time.

Carrying may sound like a lot of hard work, but it is, in fact, a really easy childcare option. If it wasn't, it simply wouldn't have survived for millions of years of human evolution. Mothers in other countries say their aim is to keep their babies alert but passive. They don't try to stimulate them too much and they certainly don't want them to cry. So they sling them into a sling and get on with their lives.

Babies all over the world go to work with their mothers, usually bound to their backs. If baby can't go to work, then he is strapped to Grandma or big sister, aunt or brother. In this way, babies are around without being the centre of attention. From the vantage point of someone's arms, the baby gets all the amusement he can take, coupled with the physical reassurance of being held. He feels like a king at the centre of his own world. He does not yet need to learn the lesson that the world does not revolve around him. He is perfectly fooled into believing that it does.

Here are some of the remarkable and unexpected effects of carrying:

- The more a baby is carried, the more his body yields and relaxes, moulding itself to your body as you move around. This limp, unresisting attitude makes the baby feel lighter at eight weeks than he does at eight days.
- The baby does not need to cry for his wants to be met. You quickly learn to interpret the wriggles that indicate hunger or a wish to change position. Mothers in other cultures can even tell when their babies are about to defecate or urinate.
- Parents often experience an unexpected and amazing sense of calmness once they start carrying a baby every-where. With my second daughter, I found I no longer had to worry whether she was awake or asleep: she managed her own timetable. I never once wondered how she was, or had to run to answer her cries. This made her infancy quite idyllic and not hard work at all.
- You are able to carry on with your own life as far as society will let you. (Few offices would actually welcome a baby, but then few babies would actually welcome an office.) Workplaces aside, there are all sorts of physical activities – housework and gardening, for instance – which are ideal for taking baby along. And meanwhile, you are all the time improving your own levels of fitness.

Want to go shopping, take a walk or meet friends for coffee? Strap baby on for the ride . . .

Did you know?

Carrying a baby around provides him with the wide-ranging stimulation he craves. In many places, this involves taking the baby to work. In South America, the Zinacantan baby relaxes to the rhythm of his mother grinding corn. Mbuti Pygmy babies in Central Africa are happy to jog along on a hunt for wild meat. Their lives could not be more different from the American or North European baby lying undisturbed in his nursery.

Rule Nine in a nutshell

- Babies love to be carried everywhere, and it really does them good.
- In cultures where carrying is normal, babies are more alert, with better motor development and balance. It is not surprising that babies cry to be cuddled and jogged around.
- The best slings are simple wraps, perhaps with extended straps, that can be moulded to your body.
- Try carrying your baby on the left-hand side to improve your subtle communications with him.
- Carrying may seem a burden, but it can be the very easiest form of childcare once you get used to it. You never have to worry about your baby or try to shoehorn him into routines. He lets you know what he needs with rarely a cry.

rule ten

Upholster your soul

'Eventually she'll cry herself to sleep. But only after she's
made the dinner, done the washing and tidied up.'
CAPTION FOR PICTURES OF A DISTRESSED
MOTHER AND BABY: NSPCC ADVERTISEMENT, 2003

Coping with crying

It's a vicious circle. Researchers tell us that babies are more
likely to cry if their mothers are depressed, or if pregnancy
and birth were difficult. Yet faced with a constantly crying
baby, the best of us become depressed. And many women
say that their difficult birth or pregnancy has ruined the
transition to motherhood.

Author Sheila Kitzinger found that women whose babies
cry more than six hours a day are more likely to have under-
gone major life changes than mothers of other babies.
Crying also increases if mothers feel bad about the birth.

So which comes first, the crying baby or the unsettled
mother? It's hard to tell in a crisis. In either case, the
struggles of early parenthood are increased when we face
them alone. We have few reference points to tell us that
crying is normal, that feeling bad about ourselves is normal
– that not coping is actually a perfectly normal feature of
parenting in Western society.

In 2002, social scientist Dr Tina Miller reported on
white, middle-class British mothers who were interviewed
before and after their babies were born. All the women had
strong ideas of what made a 'good' or 'bad' mother, yet
none of them anticipated the problems they faced when

dealing with a new baby. The poor mothers felt that any difficulties they faced were not 'normal' at all. To make matters worse, they had a powerful need to give off a positive impression of how well they were coping – even to health professionals who were there to help them.

For instance, midwives making their daily postnatal visits would say to the mothers: 'You seem to be doing fine – perhaps I won't call in tomorrow.' And what the mothers wanted to say was: 'Please come tomorrow, I depend on your visits, they support me and I feel so vulnerable and scared.' But they wouldn't say anything, because that would imply they weren't coping. At the end of the ten-day visiting period, the midwives would leave without any clue of what the mothers were really feeling.

All your life, you may have been taught that strength lies in being independent, in hiding your weaknesses. When it comes to caring for a crying baby, this feeling multiplies: we all want to avoid feelings of failure when it comes to the most important project in our life. But parents need to learn that asking for help is not a sign of weakness; admitting to problems is not an indication of failure. We cannot keep giving and coping if we are not prepared to take the help and support we need. We need to take care of ourselves.

Did you know?

Feelings of sadness following birth are called 'sakit meroyan' by mothers in rural malaysia. They say post-natal depression is brought on by powerful magic spirits surrounding the placenta. Fathers and others are expected to be especially kind to the mother during this time.

The risks of self-reliance

'. . . on a bad day, when you get very stressed, even talcum powder is abrasive.'
Clarissa Dickson Wright, television chef

The art of practically perfect parenting is to give as much as you can and no more. Your baby needs you to be strong, not burnt-out and resentful. If you are human, you will have your limits and it pays to know what they are.

The dangers of overdoing it increase when your baby cries incessantly. The baby is on full alert and so, inevitably, are his carers, the only people he can turn to. If you are your baby's primary source, then the burden can seem immense. On a good day, you may have the strength to get out of the house for a walk, meet a friend, soothe your baby's tears with a loving hug.

But on a bad day, all the negative feelings which well up inside can so easily turn into something more sinister. A wish to hurt or abandon the baby is more common than people realize. In one study, one in ten mothers admitted to shaking their crying babies or gripping them violently. And the single biggest trigger for violence is a baby who cries.

Feeling shaken yourself, it is all too easy to shake the crying baby in an effort to get him to stop. This is a useless tactic which has more to do with the parent's frustration than any calming strategy. And it can be extremely dangerous. Until recently, it was believed that babies could only be damaged by prolonged and malicious shaking, but an increase in 'shaken baby syndrome' has led to a revised warning. Up to 200 British babies – and around 3,000 American – die this way every year. Many are damaged at the hands of well-meaning parents who are stressed beyond belief.

Even moderate shaking can cause bleeding in the delicate blood vessels around the baby's brain. Doctors say the point where the brain meets the spinal cord is especially vulnerable. Most parents never mean to harm their babies, never dreamed they were capable of doing so, but find themselves stretched beyond their limits. When our thoughts get murderous or resentful, when the crying becomes too much to bear, then it's time to stop. It's time to stop the charade of self-reliance and seek help.

Did you know?

Paradoxically, you are less likely to shake or harm your baby if you carry him around on your body. The close contact of baby-wearing enhances subtle reactions and diminishes the chance of sudden or violent ones. This closeness is also helpful for mothers who feel depressed after birth, as it helps maintain the feeling of biological connection which existed during pregnancy.

Grow your own village

Don't go it alone. If there's only one message you take from this book make it this one. Surround yourself by friends and family, rely on the kindness of strangers and the willingness of neighbours. Grab a granny, adopt an aunt – do whatever you have to do to get the help you need.

All over the world, babies are brought up in community. They are not raised by one or two individuals sitting alone in a house or apartment, wondering if they are getting things right. When you are isolated with a baby, his every cough and splutter becomes a cause for concern. His crying becomes a tortuous reproach, because you are the sole person responsible for his well-being. This is not good for babies and it is certainly not good for you.

Of course babies need their mothers – and fathers – more than anyone else in the world. You will be the centre of your child's universe for at least the first seven years of his life. But babies also expect to meet the full spectrum of society: the loving, extended family who will support them and – just as importantly – support their hard-working parents. They love to be at the centre of a bustling family life, including other children and older generations, and they will happily bond with anyone who takes the time to bond with them.

In traditional villages around the world, people extend the family as far as they can. Children grow up calling every woman 'aunt' or 'mother'. Every man becomes 'uncle' or 'dad'. It's the original neighbourhood watch system and it ensures that no one feels vulnerable or alone when it comes to the crucial task of raising the new generation.

Babies may mostly have eyes for their mothers at first. But they adore being passed around by many loving hands, carried by siblings, cuddled by grandparents. And crucially, they even experience the benefits of community support through their parents' sense of well-being. When mothers are well loved and cared for, then babies have a better chance of survival.

After a baby is born in a traditional society, the complex network of community springs into action. Bands of women arrive to help care for the newly delivered mother and support the father. They get down to practical jobs like food preparation and housework. They keep unwanted visitors at bay. They protect the privacy of mother and baby so that breastfeeding can be established. They undertake important spiritual rituals to ensure that the baby's soul will stay here on earth and not try to escape back to the spirit world. Joyfully, willingly, usefully, they apply themselves to the job of post-natal pampering.

What a wonderful way to start out the journey of parenthood! Fathers find themselves involved in meaningful rituals and celebrated for their elevated status as the father of children. Mothers are given every attention, on the basis that babycare will be delivered almost entirely through her. This is the beginning of new life for families in many parts of the world – including some of the poorest countries on the map.

Here in the West, we do have support networks. We have friends and neighbours. There are queues of health professionals just waiting to assist and advise vulnerable new parents. But we don't like to admit our vulnerability and so we take hardly a fraction of what might be available for us. We talk about the value of independence, while traditional peoples talk about the value of interdependence – mutual reliance which allows them to garner support at their time of need.

If you have a new baby, then this is your time of need. Share your fears and your mistakes – everyone else has been through them too. Share the burden of a crying baby: you would be surprised how many people out there would be glad of the chance to bond with your baby for an hour a week. Recruit the teenager next door or the old lady up the road; swap an hour's childcare with a friend . . . Don't just stand there, make a village of your own.

Did you know?

Some local churches operate community care rotas to help women who have recently given birth. For a week or two, volunteers appear with freshly cooked meals, or take turns at the washing up. Look out for schemes in your area – or form your own group with mothers and pregnant friends. You could swap IOU housework tokens!

Take yourself seriously

Looking after yourself – physically and emotionally – is not an optional extra. When you have a baby to care for, it is essential to care for yourself. Here are some ideas to get you started. Many are from traditional cultures around the world, where mothers enjoy months of ritualized post-natal pampering as the natural consequence of giving birth . . .

- Prioritize yourself. You need at least half an hour a day away from the beck and call of your baby. You can do this when your baby falls asleep – but even more indulgent is to find someone to hold your baby for half an hour during the crotchety evening period. Once you are alone, take a bath, go for a walk, take a nap, meditate, read a book . . . just don't do anything remotely useful.
- Put away the polish. A little less housework can be a wonderful thing. Learn the art of Zen Dusting (i.e. letting it pile up while you sit cuddling your baby.) Try not to rush around the house cleaning every time your baby takes a nap. In many countries, women are prohibited from housework for forty days after the birth. Pin up a month-to-view calendar and give it a go! (Yes, OK, even if your baby was born six months ago . . .)

- Become a bathing beauty. Haitian women take post-natal baths strewn with castor-oil leaves. Guatemalan women enjoy ritual steam baths after giving birth. Use gentle essential oils in your bathwater to restore a feeling of well-being. A few drops of cypress or lavender oil are ideal.

- Book yourself a massage. In Polynesia, the tradition is for the new mother to lie by a fire of coconut husks while her friends massage her with coconut oil. Malaysian mothers receive twenty ritual massages in the first week or two after giving birth. If you can't afford a professional massage, ask a partner, friend or older child to rub your shoulders and feet. Children make excellent masseurs.

- Nap with your baby. Your newborn has a 'polyphasic' sleep pattern: this means he wakes and sleeps on and off all through the day and night. You – as an adult – have a 'bi-phasic' sleep pattern. This means you were designed to take a siesta. Of course, modern life doesn't often allow for such indulgences, but since you are certainly sleeping more lightly at night these days and run off your feet, this is a great time to reintroduce the habit of an afternoon sleep. If you have trouble getting off, take the baby into bed with you and let him nurse. His suckling activates a hormonal response which makes you drowsy. Before long, you'll wonder how you ever went to sleep without it.

- Eat up and enjoy! One of the joys of new parenthood is being catered for. If your partner won't do it, then you could ask your friends. Say you'd like an IOU for One Hot Meal instead of a post-natal present. Failing this, stock up with a few ready-made dinners from the supermarket before baby arrives. Post-natal meals are taken very seriously in some cultures, where mothers must observe strict food taboos and only eat the best ingredients. Indulge yourself.

- Take a sex break. In many cultures, women are not expected to resume sex while they are breastfeeding, which gives them a year or more rest from the marital role. This kind of prescription puts too much stress on the modern marriage, but you can negotiate a rest period that suits you both. Remember that 40 per cent of women still experience sexual problems three months after giving birth. The knack is to put your relationship with your partner on to the back burner without letting the light go out. Talk. Acknowledge each other's needs, even if you can't always meet them in full.

- Swallow unwanted advice with a pinch of salt. We live in a society where people are more willing to set you straight verbally than help you out practically. In societies where women receive loads of practical support, advice-giving is kept to a minimum. Whatever advice you hear, remember that you are the one who must deliver the goods. You don't have to live by anyone else's rules. Smile. Say 'How interesting,' and take time to come to your own conclusions.

Did you know?

Towards the end of her pregnancy, a Moroccan woman has her hands painted with intricate henna designs. The henna plant is imbued with baraka, a positive energy which protects mother and baby against the evil eye. As long as the patterns remain visible on her skin, the mother is exempted from all household duties, giving her at least three weeks' rest from daily chores.

Dial 999

Life with a baby is always challenging. Unless you grew up in a large family, surrounded by baby brothers and sisters, or you trained as a nursery nurse, you may have had little idea just how much disruption this cute arrival would cause. And when the cute baby cries, well, it can feel as though his despair is your despair, his pain your pain. After a few weeks of intensive baby-care, you may wonder what you ever did with all the spare time you had before the baby was born. And where, exactly, you left your self-esteem.

Just remember: your experiences are shared by most parents you meet. They may not admit it; they may put on a brilliant 'coping' face and they may look hyper-organized and capable on the exterior. But the reality will always be chequered – a tartan clash of hopes and fears, lost sleep and unexpected joys, mistakes made and hastily mended.

If you are struggling, you should refuse to struggle alone. Dial 999 to your closest friends. And if your friends aren't close enough, make a few new ones. Halve your problems by sharing them; then halve them again. Allow yourself to be emotionally rescued. Caring for your new baby takes you to the limits of your own experience. You need people to hold your hand.

You could learn the art of the coffee morning. Take time to chill out in a circle and share your own experiences. Coffee is not the point of these occasions: it's finding the community we all seek and the reassurance we crave. You will quickly learn that other parents have polarized perspectives. You cannot possibly agree with them all, or expect them all to agree with you.

While you're there, you could even start to create an atmosphere of tolerance, listening to other parents without judgment or adding your own opinion. Understand that their perspective may be different from yours. Give them the emotional support you wish for yourself.

Tolerance is the only way forward for a society which is not bound by taboos or tradition. We have the freedom to make many choices in childcare. It is always scary to new parents to be bombarded with alternative ideas and unsolicited advice. We soon learn that – since there are so many ways of raising a baby – we are never going to find the approval of all our peers. But there are advantages to the 'multiple-guess' approach. Each of us has the freedom to be ourselves.

Take every opportunity you get to support other parents in the choices they make. This way, you will teach them to respect and support you. And when you see a baby crying, make no judgments, offer no advice. All his parents want is a sympathetic smile.

Did you know?

According to recent research, 58 per cent of women describe themselves as 'depressed' six weeks after giving birth. Others use words like 'numb', or say their situation seems 'unreal'. They say they cannot communicate even to their closest friends. But new parents need to communicate and they need to start now . . .

Rule Ten in a nutshell

- Crying babies and post-natal depression often go hand-in-hand.
- Many of us simply don't realize that the problems we encounter after birth are perfectly normal and shared by most of our friends.
- We need to learn to lean on others. If we don't, we risk damaging our children and damaging ourselves.
- There are lots of ways of taking care of your own needs: some physical, some emotional. It is up to you to seek the help you need.
- If you don't live in a loving, supportive community, you can create one from the people around you. Find the support you require and the praise you deserve.

Reading list

Nikki Bradford and Jean Williams, *What They Don't Tell you about Being a Mother and Looking After Babies*, HarperCollins, London, 1997

Pat Gray, *Crying Baby – How to Cope*, Wisebuy Publications, London, 1987

Eileen Hayes, *Crying*, Practical Parenting Problem Solvers, Pan Books, London, 1999

Aletha Jauch Solter, *The Aware Baby: A new approach to parenting*, Shining Star Press, Goleta, California, 1984, revised 2001

Deborah Jackson, *Baby Wisdom: The world's best-kept secrets for the first year of parenting*, Hodder Mobius, London, 2002; *Three in a Bed*, Bloomsbury, London, 2003; *Letting Go as Children Grow*, Bloomsbury, London, 2003; *Mother and Child: The secret wisdom of pregnancy, birth and motherhood*, Duncan Baird, London, 1999

Harvey Karp, *The Happiest Baby on the Block: The new way to calm crying and help your baby sleep longer*, Bantam, London, 2003

Sheila Kitzinger, *Understanding Your Crying Baby*, Carol & Brown Publishers, 2005

Tom Lutz, 'Crying: The Natural and Cultural History of Tears, Norton & Co., New York, 1999

Anna McGrail, NCT Book of Crying Baby,Thorsons/NCT, London, 1998

Pinky McKay, 100 Ways to Calm the Crying, Lothian Books, Victoria, Australia, 2002

Ashley Montagu, Touching: The human significance of the skin, Harper & Row, New York, 1971

Desmond Morris, Illustrated Babywatching, Ebury Press, London, 1995

Jan Reynolds, Mother and Child: Visions of parenting from indigenous cultures, Inner Traditions International, Vermont, 1997

Meredith F. Small, Our Babies, Ourselves: How biology and culture shape the way we parent, Anchor Books, New York, 1999 (1998)

Dr Loraine M. Stern, Does My Child Need a Doctor?, Bloomsbury, London, 1994

D. W. Winnicott, Babies and Their Mothers, Free Association Books, London, 1988

Index